Physical Characteristics of the Black Russian Terrier

(from the American Kennel Club breed standard)

Body: The whole structure of the body should give the impression of strength.

Tail: Set high, thick and docked with 3 to 5 vertebrae left.

Hindquarters: Viewed from the rear the legs are straight and parallel, set slightly wider than the forelegs. The hindquarters are well boned and muscular with good angulation. The stifle is long and sloping. The thighs are muscular. The hocks are well let down, long and vertical when standing.

Coat: Tousled, double coat. The texture of the outer coat is coarse. The undercoat is thick and soft. Length of coat should vary from 1.5 to 4 inches and cover the entire body.

Size: Dogs at maturity are between 27 inches and 30 inches. Bitches at maturity are to be between 26 and 29 inches.

Feet Large, compact and rounded in shape. The pads of the feet are thick and firm. Nails are short and dark.

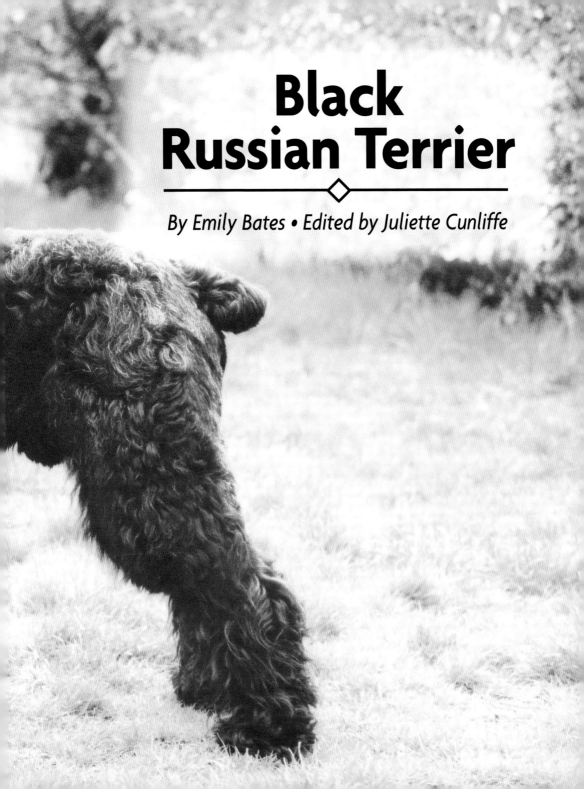

Black Russian Terrier

By Emily Bates • Edited by Juliette Cunliffe

Contents

Health Care of Your Black Russian Terrier **115**

Discover how to select a qualified vet and care for your dog at all stages of life. Topics include vaccinations, skin problems, dealing with external and internal parasites and common medical and behavioral conditions.

Showing Your Black Russian Terrier **140**

Enter the world of showing dogs. Acquaint yourself with basic show organization and handling, go beyond the conformation ring to learn about competitive performance events and meet the FCI: the "World Kennel Club."

Behavior of Your Black Russian Terrier **146**

Learn to recognize and handle behavioral problems that may arise with your Black Russian Terrier. Topics discussed include separation anxiety, aggression, barking, chewing, digging, begging, jumping up and more.

KENNEL CLUB BOOKS: **BLACK RUSSIAN TERRIER**
ISBN: 1-59378-348-5

Copyright © 2003 Kennel Club Books, Inc.
308 Main Street, Allenhurst, NJ 07711 USA
Cover Design Patented: US 6,435,559 B2 • Printed in South Korea

Photographs by Carol Ann Johnson, with additional photos by Norvia Behling, T. J. Calhoun, Carolina Biological Supply, David Dalton, Doskocil, Isabelle Francais, James Hayden-Yoav, James R. Hayden, RBP, Bill Jonas, Dwight R. Kuhn, Dr. Dennis Kunkel, Mikki Pet Products, Phototake, Jean Claude Revy, Dr. Andrew Spielman and Alice van Kempen.

The publisher wishes to thank all of the owners of the dogs featured in this book, including Sandra and John Stables.

Illustrations by Patricia Peters.

On the left is a two-and-a-half-year-old bitch from England; on the right is a four-and-a-half-year-old dog from Russia. This rare breed is gaining popularity and becoming more commonly seen around the world.

HISTORY OF THE
BLACK RUSSIAN TERRIER

The Black Russian Terrier, originally called the Black Terrier and now known by a variety of names, among them the Russkiy Tchiorny Terrier and Russian Black Terrier, is one of the youngest breeds in the world, dating back only to the 1950s. So successful has its short history been that its popularity has earned it the moniker "The Black Pearl of Russia," while many enthusiasts simply refer to the breed as the "Blackie."

The short, fascinating history of this breed is admirable and has been remarkably well documented since its beginnings. It has been said that "necessity is the mother of invention," and it is true to say that the Black Russian Terrier was born of dire necessity. Like most European countries at the close of World War II, Russia needed to rebuild itself in order to achieve both social and economic regrowth, for it was a country in ruin. The great country suffered severe losses not only among its people but also among its animals, and the most severely decimated of these animals were dogs.

Going back a little in history, after the Revolution and Civil War in Russia, from 1917 to 1923, all private Russian kennels were ruined and around 90% of pure-bred dogs were lost. The majority of those who had understood the breeding of dogs had either died or emigrated. However, in 1924, it was decided that dogs were to be used in military applications, and regional school-kennels were arranged by the Red Army in all regions, including Moscow, where the Central School-Kennel of Military Working Dogs and the Scientific Laboratory were located.

Officers were trained as instructors and trainers, and, in all forces, special departments of communication, secret services and guard services were set up. In frontier troops, there also was a department of tracking and scent hounds.

When the Great Patriotic War had begun, there were over 40,000 working dogs in Russia, with 168 separate units of working dogs that took part in battles. However, in post-war Russia, working dogs had become essentially extinct. Many stud dogs in particular were killed during the war years and the number of dogs in canine clubs was dramatically reduced. The supply simply had to be replenished, but at that time the only viable candidate was the German Shepherd Dog, which the Russians considered too aggressive (although the geographical aspect of the breed's name may also have played its part in this general aversion to the breed).

So, to replenish the supply in some other way was a gigantic task, given that, in this inhumane war, the people had experienced dreadful massacres that had left devastating effects, and the country's entire productive system had fallen apart. The people were now experiencing extreme hardship and the governors had made it clear that people must take priority over dogs.

A stalwart race, however, the Russian people recognized that if they could develop a large, strong dog with a well-balanced temperament, it would help their country in many ways. Such a dog could be used to guard agricultural areas, industrial premises and military bases. It needed to be able to function as a worker in different climatic conditions if it were to play a part in restoring the country's economy.

The Central Military School of Working Dogs, known also as the Red Star Kennel, began breeding under the leadership of Colonel G. Medvedev, with the aim of creating

a dog with all of the required characteristics. Of necessity, it had to be hardy, adaptable and easy to train, but it also had to be of substantial size, capable of performing guard work in Russia's severe climes.

Many breeds of dog were involved in the makeup of the Black Russian Terrier, most of these having been selected from the few that had survived the war in Russia. However, some, such as the Giant Schnauzer, were

MOSCOW DIVER
The Moscow Diver is one of the breeds in the background of the Black Russian Terrier. Attempts were made to develop this breed using the Caucasian Ovtcharka and Newfoundland but, according to O. Krasnovskaya, this was not a good idea. The Moscow Diver was not willing to save drowning people, but seemed to prefer to bite them! As a result, this breed was never developed.

Caucasian Ovtcharka.

imported from occupied territories. The other breeds that are familiar names to us are the Newfoundland and Rottweiler, but there were others called the Moscow Newfoundland, Moscow Great Dane and Brudasty Hound, the latter made up from the Airedale Terrier and Russian Hound. Also used was the Moscow Watchdog, which had among its ancestry the St. Bernard and the Skewbold Hound. Another breed employed was the Moscow Diver, also known as the Moscow Water Dog and Moscow Retriever, a little-known breed derived from the Newfoundland, Caucasian Sheepdog and Eastern European Sheepdog.

The crosses between the Giant Schnauzer and Airedale Terrier, like the crosses between the Rottweiler, Giant Schnauzer and Newfoundland, turned out to be very fine dogs indeed. With their black, wiry coats, they became known as Black Terriers.

It is Roy, a Giant Schnauzer, who is generally considered as the founding father of the Black Russian breed. Born in 1947, he was mated primarily to Airedale Terriers, Rottweilers and Moscow Divers, and had been selected for both his agility and his sharp guarding instinct. The Russians felt that the Airedale would impart a happy disposition, perseverance and staying power, while the Rottweiler would be valuable for its substantial construction and its courage.

Two notable males in the breed's background are Haitor, born in 1952, the result of a mating between Roy and Scotta, an Airedale, and Azart, born in 1954, resulting from a mating of Roy to Una, a Rottweiler. The Russians always selected the strongest puppies; in those early years of the breed's development, the emphasis was on producing working dogs that could both

MAKEUP OF THE BRT

According to Moscow's Dr. Eugene Tisgelnitsky, today's Black Russian Terrier (BRT) is made up of 30% Giant Schnauzer, 30% Airedale Terrier and 30% Rottweiler, and the remaining 10% is a combination of Newfoundland, Caucasian Ovcharka and East European Shepherd and Great Dane.

Airedale Terrier.

The popular Rottweiler contributed much to the Black Russian's development, including strength, substance and courage.

guard and defend and would be capable of police work. They were not selected for their beauty.

With the progression of time, it became possible to select dogs for breeding purposes that resembled each other, for the dogs were becoming more uniform, and a type could at last be set.

In 1955, the first Black Russian Terriers, these from the breed's second and third generations, took part in the Exhibition of Agricultural Achievements. All of these dogs were awarded either First- or Second-Class Diplomas. In addition, the Kennel of the Central School of Working Dogs was also awarded a Diploma. The Central School aimed to create a large, sturdily built military dog that was both hardy and strong, and Orlovsky Rusak's methods of breeding, which had been used with the Budyonovsky horse and the Estonia Hound, were used in the school's breeding program.

A couple of years later, the breed drew public attention when 40 Black Russian Terriers were exhibited at the PanSoviet Show for Police Dogs. From this time on, there was a certain collaboration between what might be described as state and private enterprise, and a few dogs that

A Black Russian Terrier with an Airedale. Although, as can be seen, many differences exist between the two breeds, the Airedale figures prominently in the BRT's background.

took part in this event were loaned to private breeders.

Kennels now began to grow and could be found not only in Moscow but also in other parts of Russia. Specialist breed clubs began to emerge and, in 1958, the first breed standard was published in *Regulations and Requirements for Training and Usage of Military Dogs*. With a breed standard to use as a guideline, it was easier for breeders to select the dogs used in their breeding programs for their typicality in breed type and conformation. This allowed them to take the breed a stage further in its development, over

and above selection solely on the basis of functional capability. That is not to say that working qualities did not continue to be improved upon, for this was also the case, but the stock certainly became more uniform in type, and hereditary faults began to disappear.

In Leningrad, there was an especially successful team of breeders under the leadership of O. Mironova, M. Shneiderovich, A. Mironov and N. Andrianova, while breeders under the leadership of M. Anokhina were successful in Moscow. J. Korepanova headed the breeders in Sverlovsk, where progress was also evident. It was not long before the Black Russian Terrier moved outside its native Russia; by the 1970s, there were over 4,000 dogs, which made this possible. The breed soon was found in the Baltic countries, the Ukraine and Siberia, Finland, Hungary, the former Czecho-slovakia and the United States.

The Black Russian Terrier was officially recognized as a breed in its homeland in 1981, with the first breed standard being offi-cially accepted on May 13 of that year by the USSR Ministry of Agriculture. It was included in Group 3 of the FCI (Fédération Cynologique Internationale, the ruling dog organization of conti-nental Europe), along with the terrier breeds proper. On many occasions, though, the Russian Kennel Club asked the FCI that the breed be moved into Group 2, along with the working breeds, where it more rightly belonged. The request was approved, thereby adding to the remarkable progress of the breed in such a short span of time. Only in France has the Black Russian Terrier remained in Group 3.

In 1984, at the World Assembly in Mexico, the International Federation of Dog-Breeding issued number 327 to the breed standard of the Black Russian Terrier. Later, in 1993, the Federation of Guard-Dog Breeding adopted the second variant of the standard, this linking in more closely to the modern-day breed. Then, in 1997, a standard was approved by the Russian Kynological Federation.

THE BREED IN ITALY

The first two Black Russian Terrier imports into Italy came in from the former Czechoslovakia in November of 1989, for there were many problems at that time surrounding the importation of the breed from Russia. These two, Cerkas z Ro-Da-Gu and Asta Nocni Boure, were in the owner-ship of Marco Galli of the Lisander Kennel. They carried Russian lines and had successful

AROUND THE WORLD
The Black Russian Terrier is now gain-ing popularity in many different coun-tries of the world. It is, indeed, remarkable how such a recently created breed has captured so much attention that is enormously geographically widespread.

show careers, with Cerkas winning the World Champion title in 1991 and 1992. In 1990, Henry Petitjean of the Spartacus Kennel brought in a male, called Char, directly from the Russian Army Kennel. The next year, from Poland, came Toro Doroi Jantros, who went on to become an Italian and International Champion.

A BRT BY ANY OTHER NAME...

This breed is now known in many parts of the world, and by numerous different names. Some of these include South Africa: Swart Russies Terrier; Bulgaria: Cheren Rouski Terrier; Czech Republic: Cerny Rusky Terier (Cerna); Denmark: Sort Russisk Terrier; England: Russian Black Terrier; Estonia: Vene must terjer; Finland: mustaterrieri; France: Terrier Noir Russe; Germany: Schwarzer Russischer Terrier; Holland: Zwarte Russische Terrier; Hungary: Orosz Fekete Terrier; Israel: Terrier Rusi Shachor; Italy: Terrier Nero Russo; Japan: Black Russian Terrier; Latvia: Melnais terjers; Norway: Sort Russisk Terrier; Spain: Terrier Ruso Negro; Sweden: Svart Terrier.

In Italy, the very first Black Russian Terrier litter was whelped on May 5, 1992 at Lisander Kennel. Sadly, there was only one puppy, and it was never shown. But the very next month, on June 10, there was another litter by the same sire, Cerkas. This litter, which is now known as the "H" litter, bred by Marco Galli, was the first Black Russian litter to make any impact on the Italian

The Black Russian usually creates quite a sensation in the ring. This dog is being shown in the Netherlands.

show scene. This litter included what were to become two Italian Champions, Hard Boy and Halloween, and the former also won the title of Youth World Champion.

There have been several other notable imports into Italy over the years, and indeed many Black Russian Terriers from Italy have made names for themselves in the show ring. The Italian organization for the breed is making great strides, and breeders in Italy generally are happy with the dogs that they are producing, with several having been exported to other countries.

THE BREED IN THE US
In the US, the Black Russian Terrier was first shown in April of 1991. This was a dog that had been imported by Roman Balfour from the Ukraine and was then sold to Louise Emmanuel.

The first specialty show for the breed was held in 1994 and comprised the largest group of Black Russian Terriers that had ever gotten together in the US.

A strong and skilled worker, the Black Russian is not all business— the breed's charm and personality shines through in all that these dogs do.

This record was not broken until the autumn of 1999.

The Black Russian is in the American Kennel Club's (AKC) Miscellaneous Class and the breed standard was approved on June 11, 2001, becoming effective on September 1 of that year. The breed is recognized by the United Kennel Club and the all-breed registry of the Continental Kennel Club. The Black Russian Terrier Club of America (BRTCA) is the national breed club in the US; this club, along with regional breed clubs, work to promote the best interests of the breed in the US.

THE BREED IN BRITAIN
In Britain, the breed is known as the Russian Black Terrier. The first of the breed to arrive in Britain was Lisander Astronomicle of Robroyd, a bitch imported from Italy, who arrived to live with Tom and Janet Huxley at the age of ten months in October of 1996. The second UK import came to Jean McDonald-Uliott the

WAR WORKERS
During the war years in the USSR, many dogs were employed in military service. They did much valuable work, including tank-fighting and mine-sniffing. They were used also to transport the seriously wounded, ammunition and food.

A Russian Black Terrier being shown with Dogues de Bordeaux in the UK. Both breeds are shown in the Imports Class.

following year. The Huxleys subsequently brought in a male from Italy's Marco Galli; this was Eestiless Joker Arbat-Roz, who arrived in December of 1997. The first litter of Russian Black Terriers to be born in the UK was owned by Peter and Louise Dudgill, and was whelped in November 1998.

A landmark in the history of the breed's representation at British shows was when the Huxleys' ten-month-old Robroyd Russkoe Zoloto took Best Puppy in Show at Ireland's prestigious St. Patrick's Day All-Breed International Championship Show in March 2000. This was quite a feat for a breed that had only made its first appearance in this part of the world a few years earlier.

The Russian Black Terrier Club (UK) was formed in

December of 1998, and was officially recognized by England's Kennel Club in May 2000. The Kennel Club accepted the Interim Breed Standard on September 1, 2000. This standard had been based on the Russian standard, though of necessity it had to be drawn up in line with the format used for all of the Kennel Club's breed standards.

April 22, 2001 marked the official launch of the Russian Black Terrier in the UK. Many owners, enthusiasts and judges joined together at Wentworth Castle in Yorkshire, England to absorb as much information as possible about the breed. Of particular interest was the lineup of the Russian Black Terrier, Giant Schnauzer and Bouvier des Flandres, three breeds that can cause confusion to the novice eye.

CHARACTERISTICS OF THE

BLACK RUSSIAN TERRIER

Apart from the breed's striking good looks, the Black Russian Terrier, fondly known as the "Blackie," has remarkable working abilities coupled with strength and courage. While these are indeed wonderful abilities, they do not make him the ideal dog to fit in with all family situations. It should be borne in mind that the breed was first developed as a working dog, but it has changed over time, both physically and temperamentally. Therefore, it is sensible to look back briefly over the decades to see how this has happened.

The breed in the 1960s and 1970s was generally larger and sometimes more well boned than it is today. Dogs then had hard, wiry coats; the longer, softer coats were penalized as faults. The breed's temperament in the early years was considerably more difficult than it is today, with the breed being difficult for the average person to handle. That being said, in the right hands, if expertly trained, these dogs were quite remarkable animals, as had been proven in the military training schools.

DOGS, DOGS, GOOD FOR YOUR HEART!

People usually purchase dogs for companionship, but studies show that dogs can help to improve their owners' health and level of activity, as well as lower a human's risk of coronary heart disease. Without even realizing it, when a person puts time into exercising, grooming and feeding a dog, he also puts more time into his own personal health care. Dog owners establish more routine schedules for their dogs to follow, which can have positive effects on their own health. Dogs also teach us patience, offer unconditional love and provide the joy of having a furry friend to pet!

As the breed expanded in number, many Black Russian Terriers in their homeland had to live in apartments in large cities. It was therefore essential that breeders took this into consideration when breeding the dogs; thus, they were in some measure adapted for "modern living."

PERSONALITY

Today's Black Russian Terrier is temperamentally sound, although the breed does have a natural guarding instinct, a fact of which we should always be aware. This is a brave and self-confident dog, with an alert, lively and even temperament, though he is usually rather wary of strangers.

Indeed the "Blackie" is quite capable of taking on an intruder or a stranger, so this aspect of the dog's character should be kept under close supervision when visitors arrive at your home, especially if the visitors are unexpected. Some believe that if the Blackie could speak, he would say, "Don't touch me or my family, and I'll leave you in peace."

As a pet, the Black Russian is wonderfully devoted to his owners and is usually good with children, but it is always important to supervise young children with dogs, regardless of the animal's size and strength. This is a substantially built dog, and it is always possible that an accident may happen, even if only by way of the dog's accidentally bowling over a child. Both child and dog must be taught to respect each other, and a dog must always be allowed his own space when he needs a little peace and quiet. It is also worth keeping in mind that a Black Russian Terrier may decide to protect a child if he thinks the child to be in danger of any sort, especially if approached by someone with whom the dog is not familiar. There have also been occasions when the breed has

THE BLACKIE'S MANY JOBS

Black Russian Terriers have been used not only as prison guardians and all-around military and police dogs but also as sled dogs. They have had some success in this field and perform better at sledding than many other working dogs, but their expertise cannot be compared to that of breeds such as the Siberian Husky. A few Blackies have also been used as cattle drivers and as flock herders.

In Russia, the breed is now growing in popularity among farmers. The Blackie is a good guard dog, and he is difficult to see in the darkness because of his black coat. He is said to be fast and silent, like a ghost. The Black Russian Terrier is highly suitable for guarding large open territories because he is extremely watchful, though he is never cruel to cattle and has not been known to attack anyone who is not an intended target.

SENSITIVE SIDE

The Black Russian Terrier seems to have the ability to analyze a situation and to adapt to it without any great problem. He has a well-developed sensitivity and a desire to understand and carry out his owner's wishes. A description that many owners feel appropriate for this breed is that Black Russian Terriers are "people in fur," though a pedant might prefer to think of them as "people in hair."

been known to "herd" up a group of children!

In general, the breed is not known for its dominant character, although there are exceptions, particularly in males. Males often tend to be more dominant and show concern for their own dignity. They can be easier to socialize but, while maturing, often try to challenge their owners' dominant position in the household. The male likes to test his owner's boundaries to see how much will be tolerated. Females are often more loving with their owners and can be more distrustful of strangers. They are more likely to accept that the head of the household is "top dog." Another distinction is that dogs generally are larger than bitches but, because the breed is still varied in size, this is not always the case.

The Black Russian Terrier is very adaptable and is easily

Although a large breed, the BRT is very adaptable and enjoys life in the home with his family—but don't let your Blackie become a couch potato!

trained, but, if he finds himself or his owner in a dangerous situation, he can react very quickly. An owner or handler of a Black Russian must always be aware of this. Because of the breed's guarding instincts and wariness of strangers, careful training and socialization are important from a young age. This is important for all situations, and those who plan to show their Blackies will need to pay special attention to these aspects if the dogs are to behave well in the show ring among the distractions of many unfamiliar

Owners and their Blackies most often see "eye-to-eye."

people and dogs. Compared with some other breeds, though, the Black Russian Terrier is not a fighter when it comes to other dogs, and rarely will challenge another dog first.

There is no exception to the rule that a Black Russian Terrier must be trained, but this is a very particular dog that requires expert handling with extreme sensitivity. It is generally acknowledged that strong, coercive training methods can be damaging and do not work for this breed. It is important to qualify that when I talk of "training," I mean only in the general sense (basic commands, good behavior, etc.). Any form of protection training, if given, should not commence until the dog is one-and-a-half to two years of age.

In short, today's Black Russian Terrier is best as a family dog, and is better suited to a household

environment than to a kennel situation. This is certainly not a breed that will accept being chained up or kept outdoors only. In whatever situation they are kept, companionship and social-ization is of the utmost impor-tance, along with the opportunity to exercise. A Black Russian Terrier both enjoys and needs the company of his owner when enjoying a healthy long walk.

PHYSICAL CHARACTERISTICS

The Black Russian Terrier is a sizeable dog, large and imposing in both weight and substance. Strongly built with massive bone, the almost square body has a sturdy, robust frame with well-developed muscles. Long-bodied dogs, or those that are narrow all through, are highly untypical of the breed.

The chest is deep and the ribs well sprung, and there is only a moderate tuck-up. This could be described as a "deep-bodied" dog. The feet are large, well arched and rounded, and it is important that they have thick pads beneath. No Black Russian Terriers should have hind dewclaws, as they are to be removed.

Another important feature of the breed is that the withers are high and clearly marked above the topline. The reasonably long, powerful neck is muscular and clean-cut.

The high-set tail on the Black

Above: The BRT's facial furnishings—the heavy eyebrows, mustache and beard—are trademarks of the breed.

Yes, there are eyes under all of that hair! Some owners like to tie the hair up to keep it out of their dogs' faces.

Russian Terrier is customarily docked, leaving three to five vertebrae, but it also can be left undocked. In Russia, however, an undocked tail is a disqualifying fault. In the case of an undocked tail, the set of the tail is more important than its carriage and, while it may be carried over the back, it should not be carried gaily.

HEAD AND EARS

The skull is moderately broad, the head is well proportioned and the cheekbones are rounded. The skull is flat, and the topline of the skull should be parallel to the topline of the muzzle. The dense whiskers and beard give the muzzle a squared-off shape.

The pigmentation of nose, eye rims and lips is black, and the thick lips should be tightly fitting and not pendulous. In keeping

with the color of the breed, the medium-sized, oval eyes are dark and set obliquely, wide apart.

The ears are pendant and not too large, but are high-set. Their shape is triangular, so that the inner edge lies against the bone of the cheek.

Given the original function of the Black Russian Terrier, it should go without saying that the jaws must be strong, and a scissors bite with full dentition is required. In Russia, the bite is considered as one of the biggest problems with modern-day breeding because many of the breed's ancestors had problems in this area.

SIZE

I have already stressed that the Black Russian Terrier is a strongly built dog of above-average size, and owners selecting any large breed of dog should consider this very carefully from the outset. Not only will a large breed require more room around the house, the dog also will need more space and time for exercise, and will cost considerably more to feed than a smaller breed.

In general, dogs are larger than bitches, and exact measurements vary slightly among the various standards. The Russian standard states that a dog's height should be 27–29 inches, while the AKC standard allows 27–30 inches. Likewise in bitches, the

THE BOUNCY BLACKIE

The Black Russian Terrier, though large, is a highly agile breed. One owner describes her 30-inch-tall dog, who weighs 145 lbs, "like a basketball when he bounces on and off a picnic table." Another is known to be able to jump 5 feet straight up in the air.

Russian requirement is 26–28 inches and the AKC's is 26–29 inches. In Russia, what they describe as the "old-fashioned" Blackies can sometimes measure up to 31.5 inches, and they have more bone and substance than the more modern type.

MOVEMENT

When at the trot, the legs of this breed move in a straight line, although the forelegs converge just slightly. The dog covers the ground well, with good reach in front and good driving power from behind, and the movement shows some elasticity. This is particularly necessary for a breed of such size and weight, for it should be able to jump high and quickly change speed and direction. Although not written in the breed standard, it should be possible to see the full footpads as the dog moves away.

COAT AND COLOR

The breed has a weatherproof coat with a dense undercoat. It is not wiry or soft and, when the hair is brushed, it is broken-coated and slightly waved. However, the coat in the breed is not the same harsh coat as in the original standard, and currently moves are underway to revise this section of the standard.

There are good furnishings on the eyebrows, beard and legs;

Differences in coat type: the top picture shows the old-fashioned, shorter, wiry coat; the bottom picture shows the longer coat, in which the hair is softer and wavy.

indeed, in the early days in Russia, the Blackie had hair rising up on the brows, but this is not favored by exhibitors now. In Russia, any dogs without decorative hair, beard or mustache are always penalized.

As the breed is such a young one, and bearing in mind that it has developed from several breeds, it is understandable that coats still vary to some extent. According to Dr. Tisgelnitsky in Russia, there are two main types: the old-fashioned wire-coated type, sometimes called the "short-coated Blackie," and the modern longer-coated type, with softer, wavy hair. He points out, though, that the coat must provide satisfactory protection from the weather and should be rather rough. Soft, short, silky hair and curly hair are listed as disqualifying faults in the Russian standard. Dr. Tisgelnitsky says that the two types may be either crossbred or bred separately, but that the majority of show champions are of the longer-coated variety.

Black Russian Terriers do shed, certainly not as much as many breeds, but you must be prepared for some shedding around the home nonetheless.

It is not surprising that the only accepted color for the breed is black, but a dog can be black with an insignificant amount of gray hairs. In Russia, some people involved with only working dogs

BASIC TRAINING
A typical Black Russian Terrier is a reliable, temperamentally well-balanced dog that is only aggressive when he actually needs to be. Nonetheless, sensible training is of the utmost importance. Teaching the dog to be obedient to your commands is the basis of all training.

and not show dogs are experimenting by breeding bloodlines with a silver-gray color, but it is stressed that this is not a color that is approved in the FCI, Russian, American or British breed standards.

HEALTH CONSIDERATIONS

In general, the Black Russian Terrier is a healthy dog. As with all breeds, though, there are certain health problems that need to be addressed. After all, it is in the best interest of the breed for potential owners to know what to look out for. If owners are aware of the problems that can occur, they are undoubtedly in a position to deal with them in the best manner possible. Some conditions are genetic and thus carried via heredity, but others are not.

As the Black Russian Terrier is such a newly developed breed, it is always worth keeping in mind that the incidence of many health problems can be decreased over time by selective breeding.

HIP DYSPLASIA

The Black Russian Terrier is predisposed to hip dysplasia, as are many of the larger, heavier breeds. It is therefore strongly recommended, in order to eliminate dysplastic dogs from breeding programs, that the appropriate x-ray testing be done. HD detection schemes, in which dog's hip rays are evaluated and the dog's

DO YOU KNOW ABOUT HIP DYSPLASIA?

Hip dysplasia is a condition sometimes found in Black Russian Terriers, as well as in other breeds. When a dog has hip dysplasia, his hind leg has an incorrectly formed hip joint. By constant use of the hip joint, it becomes more and more loose, wears abnormally and may become arthritic.

Hip dysplasia can only be confirmed with an x-ray, but certain symptoms may indicate a problem. Your Black Russian Terrier may have a hip dysplasia problem if he walks in a peculiar manner, hops instead of smoothly running, uses his hinds legs in unison (to keep the pressure off the weak joint), has trouble getting up from a prone position and always sits with both legs together on one side of his body. As the dog matures, he may adapt well to life with a bad hip, but in a few years the arthritis develops and many Black Russian Terriers with hip dysplasia become crippled. Hip dysplasia is considered an inherited disease and can be definitely diagnosed by x-ray when the dog is two years old.

Some experts claim that a special diet might help your puppy outgrow the bad hip, but the usual treatments are surgical. The removal of the pectineus muscle, the removal of the round part of the femur, reconstructing the pelvis and replacing the hip with an artificial one are some treatment options. All of these surgical interventions are expensive, but they are usually very successful. Follow the advice of your veterinarian.

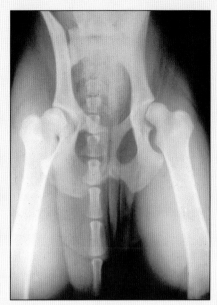

X-ray of "moderate" dysplastic hips.

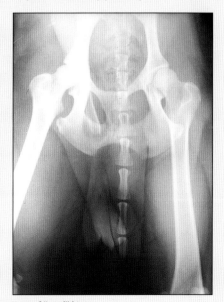

X-ray of "good" hips.

Compare the two hip joints and you'll understand dysplasia better. Hip dysplasia is a badly worn hip joint caused by improper fit of the bone into the socket. It is easily the most common hip problem in dogs.

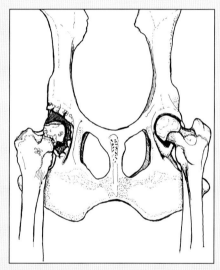

Above: The healthy hip joint on the right and the unhealthy hip joint on the left.

Hip dysplasia can only be positively diagnosed by x-ray. Dogs usually manifest the problem when they are between four and nine months of age, the so-called fast growth period, although a dog cannot be determined to be clear of or affected by hip dysplasia until he is two years old.

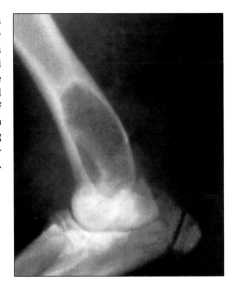

X-ray of a dog's elbow. X-ray testing schemes are essential tools in the gradual elimination of dysplasia through selective breeding of dysplasia-free dogs.

hips are graded, are available in many countries. These grading or scoring systems determine whether a dog is free of dysplasia or affected and, if so, to what degree, thus determining whether a dog is suitable or unsuitable for breeding.

HD is a problem involving the malformation of the ball-and-socket joint at the hip, a developmental condition caused by the interaction of many genes. This results in looseness of the hip joints and, although not always painful, HD can cause lameness and can impair typical movement. Although a dog's environment does not actually cause hip dysplasia, it may have some bearing on how unstable the hip joint eventually becomes. Osteoarthritis eventually develops as a result of the instability.

ELBOW DYSPLASIA

A similar form of dysplasia can occur in the elbow of the Black Russian Terrier. This can affect a dog quite suddenly and can cause lameness, with arthritis usually resulting in the elbow joint. As with hip dysplasia, elbows can be x-rayed to determine if a dog is affected and the severity; those that are affected should be eliminated from breeding programs.

BLOAT/GASTRIC TORSION

Gastric torsion, more commonly called "bloat," is a potentially deadly condition that can affect any breed, but the deep-chested breeds run the greatest risk. This is a condition in which the stomach twists around on itself, preventing any gases or stomach contents from leaving. Blood supply is cut off as well, and shock, and eventually death, usually results very rapidly. Fortunately, there are many preventative measures that an owner can take to protect his dog from bloat; these are discussed in more detail in the health chapter.

OBESITY

It is always prudent to keep a careful eye on your Black Russian's weight, for any excess weight can contribute to health problems.

TEETH

It is important to pay close attention to the care of your Blackie's teeth and gums so that they remain as healthy as possible, thereby preventing decay, infection and resultant loss. Feeding dry foods is recommended by many as a means of helping to keep teeth clean and in good condition. Of course, regular careful brushing with a veterinary toothpaste can help enormously.

If you notice signs of infection in your dog's gums, it must be dealt with promptly, for the infection may not just stop at the gums. The bacteria can be carried through the bloodstream, the result of which can be diseases of the liver, kidney, heart and joints. This is all the more reason to realize that efficient dental care is of utmost importance throughout a dog's life.

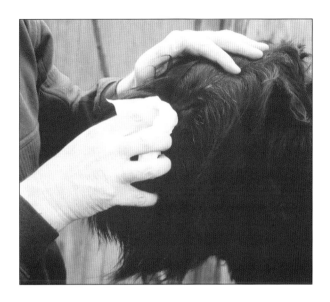

EYES

It is particularly important to be watchful about the cleanliness and condition of your dog's eyes, so as to avoid eye infections' arising. At the first sign of infection or injury, especially if the eye is starting to turn blue in color, urgent veterinary attention is required. Early diagnosis and treatment can often save a dog's sight. It is advisable to have your Black Russian Terrier's eyes tested every year as a preventative measure.

The BRT is one of the breeds that carries coat over its eyes, a feature designed for protective purposes. However, long hair over a dog's eyes can cause irritation, which can have long-term effects, such as the occurrence of "dry eye" in old age. This makes eye

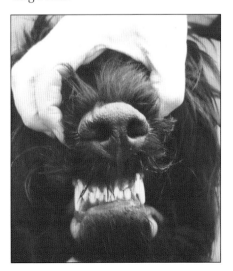

Above: The long facial furnishings make it necessary for you to pay special attention to your BRT's eyes. The area around the eyes should be kept clean, and you must check the eyes often for any sign of irritation.

A correct bite and healthy mouth in an adult Black Russian Terrier. Home dental care is as important for your Blackie as it is for you.

Provide your BRT with the best care and attention from puppyhood, and he will provide you with unmatched loyalty and devotion throughout his life.

care for the Black Russian of particular significance.

HEART PROBLEMS
Occasionally dogs can suffer heart problems, particularly as they become more advanced in age. Heart checks should of course be a part of your Blackie's routine examinations, but it is wise to ask the vet to check the dog's heart whenever you visit, for whatever reason (although many vets will do this automatically.)

HEAT EXHAUSTION
Frequently, people do not realize how quickly death can result from heat exhaustion in dogs. The first sign is the dog's heavy panting, and he begins to puff or gasp for air. When walking, the dog appears dizzy and tends to weave, subsequently collapsing with eventual unconsciousness.

At the first sign of heat exhaustion, the dog should be taken out of the sun and water offered to him. His body should be doused in water, especially the head and neck. If available, ice bags or even a package of frozen vegetables should be placed around his head and neck. Because it is urgently necessary to lower the dog's body temperature, these things should be done even before taking your dog to a vet.

WHO'S WHO?
The Black Russian Terrier is sometimes confused with the Giant Schnauzer and Bouvier des Flandres, particularly by those who are unfamiliar with these three breeds. An easy comparison to make is that if the Bouvier is a "heavy athlete" and the Giant Schnauzer is a "runner," the Black Russian Terrier falls somewhere in the middle and might be described as an "all-around sportsman."

Giant Schnauzer.

Bouvier des Flandres.

BLACK RUSSIAN TERRIER

A breed standard is a written description of the ideal characteristics of a given breed, both physically and temperamentally. It is essentially a "word picture" of the breed. A breed standard undoubtedly helps breeders to produce stock that comes as close as possible to the recognized ideal, and helps judges to know exactly what they are looking for in selecting their winners. By adhering to the breed standard, essential characteristics of the breed are preserved over the generations, ensuring consistency in type and preserving the traits that make the breed what it is.

It is important for enthusiasts to study the standard carefully, and even more beneficial to couple this with practical experience of assessing a dog. Only in this way can you fully digest the finer points of the breed. There are various points of any breed standard that are easy to gloss over without much thought, but it

Profile showing the correct type, balance, structure and substance with mature coat, trimmed to show off coat and structure.

is these fine points that help to make the breed what it is. For example, you will notice that not only is the Black Russian Terrier's rump to be wide and muscular but there also should be a slight slope toward the tail, which is set high on the croup. It is descriptions such as these that a fancier needs to absorb in order to truly understand the construction of the breed.

Of course, while all breed standards are designed effectively to paint a picture in words, each reader, judge and breeder will almost certainly have a slightly different way of interpreting these words. After all, were everyone to interpret a breed's standard in exactly the same way, there would only be one consistent winner within the breed at any given time!

In any event, to fully comprehend the intricacies of a breed, reading words alone is never enough. In addition, it is essential for devotees to watch Black Russian Terriers being judged at shows and, if possible, to attend seminars at which the breed is discussed. Owners of this relatively new breed are a highly enthusiastic crowd and they always seem willing to share their knowledge.

Breed standards can vary from country to country and registry to registry. It is interesting to look at the Russian standard, as this is the standard of the breed's home-

Head study, showing correct type, balance, structure and substance.

land. The Russian Kynological Federation standard is presented here, followed by the standard of the American Kennel Club, of which the breed became a member of the Miscellaneous Class in 2001.

THE RUSSIAN BREED STANDARD
The following breed standard for Black Russian Terriers was approved in 1997 by the Russian Kynological Federation Standards Commission, the Russian Kynological Federation Presidium and the Cattle and Breeding Bureau of the Ministry of Agricultural Products of the Russian Federation. The following

BREEDING CONSIDERATIONS
The decision to breed your dog is one that must be considered carefully and researched thoroughly before moving into action. Some people believe that breeding will make their bitches happier or that it is an easy way to make money. Unfortunately, indiscriminate breeding only worsens the rampant problem of pet overpopulation, as well as putting a considerable dent in your pocketbook. As for the bitch, the entire process from mating through whelping is not an easy one and puts your pet under considerable stress. Last, but not least, consider whether or not you have the means to care for an entire litter of pups. Without a reputation in the field, your attempts to sell the pups may be unsuccessful.

is a translation of that standard as it originally appeared in "Vestnik RKF" No. 4, 1997.

The Black Russian Terrier is a dog of above-average and large size, strong, enduring, courageous, self-confident, with a square or slightly stretched frame, easily adaptable to different climatic conditions, and well trainable. Many years of using the Black Terrier as a watchdog prove his high efficiency and reliability. Balanced temperament and good trainability allow to him to be used not only as a guard dog but also in other kinds of work.

The Black Russian Terrier has massive bone structure, proportionate sturdy and rough build, heavy musculature. Type of temperament is stable-agile with defensive reaction in active form. Sex type must be well pronounced.

Height of males is 68–74 cm (27–29 in), for females 66–72 cm (26–28 in). Lower height limit for males is 66 cm (26 in), females 64 cm (25 in). The upper limit can be exceeded by 3 cm (1.25 in). Deviation from the desirable height (the upper limit) by more than 3 cm significantly decreases the breeding value of the dog.

The whole body of the Black Russian Terrier is covered with a thick, rough coat. Decorative hair is well developed (on the head and limbs). Trimming is obligatory in accordance with approved style.

The Black Russian Terrier was developed in The Red Star Kennel by the crossing of proven and compatible working breeds: Giant Schnauzer, Airedale Terrier, Rottweiler, Newfoundland.

Head: Proportionate to the overall build, long (equals or slightly exceeds 40% of dog's height at the withers), with moderately wide skull, rounded but not too pronounced cheekbones, superciliary arches well developed. The forehead is flat, stop is defined but not steep, top of the skull and muzzle are parallel. Muzzle is massive, slightly tapering to the nose, slightly shorter than half of the length of the head. Mustache and beard give the muzzle a blunt rectangular shape, lips are thick, fleshy, black, tight and without flews. Nose is large and black. The gums have dark pigmentation.

Ears: Set high, hanging on the cartilage, rather small, triangular in shape, with front edge lying close to the cheeks. The hanging part of the ear is firm without dents or folds.

Eyes: Rather small, oval shaped, set straight and wide, dark. Eyelids are dry, dark and tight.

Teeth: Large, white, set close to each other, with full dentition (42 teeth). Incisors form a straight line at the base. Scissors bite.

Neck: Massive, of medium length (approximately equals to the length of the head), dry, muscular. Set at 40–45-degree angle to the line of the back.

Body: The chest is deep, long, wide, in cross section has oval shape, with slightly prominent ribs. Forechest is slightly protruding in relation to the point of shoulder. Lower part of the chest is level with the elbows or a little below. Depth of the chest is about 46–47% of dog's height. Withers

Frontal head study, showing the width of skull, large nose and abundant facial furnishings.

are high, long, well developed, pronounced. Height at the withers exceeds the height at the croup by 1–2 cms (0.5–1 in). Back is strong, straight, wide, muscular. Length of the back is approximately half of the distance from point of withers to the base of the tail. Loin is short (about half of the length of

In profile, the head shows a flat forehead, massive muzzle and defined stop.

the back), wide, muscular, slightly prominent. The croup is wide, muscular, moderately long, slightly sloping toward the highly set tail.

Tail: Set high, thick, docked short (three to five vertebrae left).

Forelegs: Straight and parallel when viewed from the front. Shoulder blades are long, sloping at a 45-degree angle. Angle between the shoulder blade and upper arm is about 100 degrees. Upper arms are muscular. Arms are straight, thick, of medium length, vertical and parallel to each other, elbows are pointed back. Pasterns are short, massive, almost vertical. Length of the front leg to the elbow is about 53–54% of dog's height.

Hindquarters: From rear view, legs are straight and parallel, set slightly wider than the forelegs. Upper thighs are long, sloping at about a 100-degree angle. Thighs are long, slanting, pasterns are vertical, of moderate length. Angulation of stifles and hocks is pronounced.

Paws: Paws are large, compact, rounded in shape. Nails are dark. Rear dewclaws must be removed.

Coat: Hair coat is rough and thick. Hair with fold, 4–10 cm (2–4 in) long, covers the whole body.

Decorative hair is well developed, forming the eyebrows, the mustache (whiskers) and the beard on the head. Front and rear legs are well protected by long rough hair. Undercoat is thick, soft, well developed. Mandatory trimming according to approved style.

Color: The color is black, or black with insignificant amount of gray hair.

Movement: Characteristic gait is non-overreaching trot or canter. At the trot, legs must move straight with front legs stepping slightly closer to the middle line, back and loin springing elastically. Joints of front and rear limbs open freely. In motion, dog covers a lot of ground, which is caused by a strong push of the hindquarters and significant reaching out of the forelegs.

Major Faults: Deviation toward light or raw built, high or low on legs, stretched frame. Sluggishness or excessive excitability. Short, rough, light, heavy, out of proportion head. Round skull, very pronounced cheeks. Short, snub, lowered, narrow, chiseled muzzle, raw lips (flews), small nose. Wrinkled, semi-erect ears, ears not touching the cheek. Round, light-colored, slant or narrow-set eyes. Small, widely spaced, badly damaged teeth.

FAULTS IN PROFILE

Heavy loaded and upright shoulders, low on leg, over-angulated behind, tail not carried properly.

Generally lacking substance, ewe necked, pinched front and toes out in front, lacking angulation in front and rear, weak rear, dip behind shoulders, steep in croup, low tailset and large ears.

Upright shoulders, long back, weak rear, straight behind, low tailset.

Short neck, upright and loaded shoulders, sloping topline, weak rear and lacking angulation.

Front view of a BRT gaiting, showing ease and effortlessness of movement.

Short high-set neck, dewlap. Flat, barrel-shaped, shallow, "open," narrow chest. Soft, narrow, arching back. Long, hanging, arching, narrow loin. Horizontal, sloping, narrow croup. Curled tail. Straight or sharp shoulder. Legs set too narrow. Short upper or lower thighs, raw joints. Extreme or insufficient angulation of hindquarters. Flat, spread paws, light-colored nails, rear dewclaws. Gray color of over one-third of the coat. Straight, closelying hair on the body even in combination with decorative hair on the head and legs. Tied-up, heavy gaits, during movement croup is higher than withers, swaying of the croup, crab-like motion, pacing.

Disqualifying Faults: Non-proportionate build. Deviation from correct type of build. Shyness, excessive excitability, uncontrolled aggressiveness. Unilateral or bilateral cryptorchidism, underdeveloped testicles. Nose not black. All deviation from scissors bite, lack of any teeth, incisors not lined up at the base. Undocked tail. Soft, short, silky hair, curly hair. Lack of decorative hair on the head and legs. White spots and marks. Clearly defined areas of profound gray hair. Non-standard color.

THE AMERICAN KENNEL CLUB STANDARD FOR THE BLACK RUSSIAN TERRIER (MISCELLANEOUS CLASS)

History: During the 1930s a military kennel named the Red Star started work on a native breed that would be part of the

BREEDER'S BLUEPRINT
If you are considering breeding your bitch, it is very important that you are familiar with the breed standard. Reputable breeders breed with the intention of producing dogs that are as close as possible to the standard and that contribute to the advancement of the breed. Study the standard for both physical appearance and temperament, and make certain your bitch and your chosen stud dog measure up.

national security force.

The Red Star Kennel worked on selective interbreeding using Rottweiler, Giant Schnauzer, Airedale and Newfoundland mixes. It was important to have a large breed not only reliable but trainable in many different situations. The dog would also have to be able to endure the harsh Russian winters.

By 1956 it finally reached the point where the Black Russian Terrier bred true. In 1981 The Russian Ministry of Agriculture recognized the breed and it was internationally accepted by the FCI in 1984.

General Appearance: The Black Russian Terrier (BRT) is a robust, large and powerful dog. The dog has large bone and well-developed muscles. The breed was developed in Russia and used as guard dogs for protection. They must be balanced, have a good temperament and be reliable. The dogs have great courage and strength. They are capable of endurance. Dogs must have a large frame and heavy bone.

Side view of gait, showing reach and drive, enabling the dog to cover much ground with each stride.

Bitches are definitely to appear feminine but never lacking in substance.

Size, Proportion, Substance: Size: Dogs at maturity are between 27 inches and 30 inches. Bitches at maturity are to be between 26 and 29 inches. A deviation from the ideal height is to be faulted. *Any dog or bitch under 26 inches is a disqualification.* **Proportion:** The Black Russian Terrier is slightly longer than tall. The most desired proportions are 9.5 to 10. The length is measured from breastbone to rear edge of the pelvis.

MEETING THE IDEAL

The American Kennel Club defines a standard as: "A description of the ideal dog of each recognized breed, to serve as an ideal against which dogs are judged at shows." This "blueprint" is drawn up by the breed's recognized parent club, approved by a majority of its membership and then submitted to the AKC for approval. The AKC states that "An understanding of any breed must begin with its standard. This applies to all dogs, not just those intended for showing." The picture that the standard draws of the dog's type, gait, temperament and structure is the guiding image used by breeders as they plan their programs.

Head: The head must be in proportion to the body. It should give the appearance of power and strength. **Eyes:** The eyes should be of medium size and dark. Eye rims are to be black without sagging or prominent haw. The eye is to be oval shaped. Light eyes are a serious fault. **Ears:** The ears are set high and are rather small and triangular in shape. The front edge of the ear should lie close to the cheek. The length of the ear should reach the outside corner of the eye. Ears set low on the skull are to be faulted. Cropped ears are not acceptable. The head should be powerfully built with a moderately broad and blocky **skull.** Viewed from the side, it should appear balanced. The head is made of two parallel planes. The back skull to muzzle is measured from the corner of the eye. Occiput should be well developed. The **muzzle** should be slightly shorter than the back skull. The length of the muzzle to the back skull is approximately a ratio of 4 to 5. The forehead must be flat with a marked but not pronounced stop. The head of the male is distinctly masculine, and that of the bitch, distinctly feminine. **Nose:** The nose must be large and black. *Disqualification: Nose other than black.* **Lips:** are full, tight and black. There are to be no flews. The gums have dark pigmentation. Black mark on the tongue is allowed. **Teeth:** The

In the show ring, the judge evaluates each dog's conformity to its breed standard. Part of the judging is "hands-on," as the judge feels underneath the coat for correct structure.

teeth are large and white. There should be full dentition. The incisors form a straight line at the base. The bite should be scissors. Any missing teeth are a serious fault. *Undershot or overshot bites are a disqualification.*

Neck, Topline, and Body:
Neck: The neck should be thick, muscular and powerful. Length is not to be excessive. There should be no pendulous or excessive dewlap. The length of the neck and the length of the head should be approximately the same. An excessively thick neck is considered a fault. **Body:** The whole structure of the body should give the impression of strength. The **chest** is deep and wide. The shape should be oval and reach to the elbows or a little below. The withers are high, pronounced and well developed. The topline is level and straight. The **loin** is short. The abdomen is well tucked up and firm. Withers are higher than and sloping into the level back. **Croup** is wide, muscular, moderately long, slightly sloping toward the high tail set. **Tail** is set high, thick

and docked with three to five vertebrae left. An undocked tail is not to be penalized.

Forequarters: Shoulders should be large and muscular, well developed with blades broad and sloping. The shoulders should be well laid back. The angle between the shoulder blades and the upper arm is at a 100 to 110 degree. Shoulders are well muscled. The forelegs are straight and well boned. The elbows must turn neither in nor out while standing or moving. The forelegs are straight and muscular. Pasterns are short and almost vertical. Length of the front leg to the elbow should be about 53 to 54% of the dog's height. **Feet** are large, compact, and rounded in shape. The pads of the feet are thick and firm. Nails are short and dark. Rear dewclaws could be removed.

Hindquarters: Viewed from the rear, the legs are straight and parallel, set slightly wider than the forelegs. The hindquarters are well boned and muscular with good angulation. The stifle is long and sloping. The thighs are muscular. The hocks are well let down, long and vertical when standing.

Coat: Tousled, double coat. The texture of the outer coat is coarse. The undercoat is thick and soft. Length of coat should vary from 1.5 to 4 inches and cover the entire body. It is a pronounced tousled coat rather than wiry or curly.

Presentation: Presentation of the breed in the show ring, the dog's outline is clearly defined. The dogs will be trimmed but should not appear to be sculpted. Ears: Hair should be trimmed inside and outside the ear. The ears will lay flat to the side of the head. Forehead: Just behind the eyebrows the hair is to be shaved or cut very short so as to make what appears to be a platform. The rest of the forehead is trimmed so that the shorter hairs will blend with the longer hairs of the muzzle. This forms a "cap" which should help define length of backskull. Looking from the top of the head, it should give the appearance of a "brick." The fringe from the eyebrows is brushed forward and blends with the beard and muzzle. This blending of hair should look from the side like a "triangle." Neck: The front of the neck from the throat to the point of shoulder should be shaved or scissored short. The hair on the back of the neck should appear to have a mane down to the withers. Topline: Trimmed from the withers to the tail so that when viewed from the side it appears level. The hair from the back should then blend down the sides of the dog. It is stressed that there should be no distinct lines or scissors marks.

The overall impression of the Black Russian Terrier is that of a massive, sturdy, powerful dog.

Color: The only acceptable colors for the Black Russian Terrier is black or black with a few gray hairs. *Any other color is to be considered a disqualification.*

Gait: A Black Russian Terrier should move freely with a smooth easy springy motion. The motion should be well-balanced and fluid. As the Black Russian Terrier moves faster, the feet will converge toward a centerline. The topline should remain level.

Temperament: The character and temperament of the Black Russian Terrier is of utmost importance. The Black Russian Terrier is a calm, confident and courageous dog with a self-assurance which sometimes is rather aloof toward strangers. They are highly intelligent, extremely reliable. They were bred to guard and protect. The behavior in the show ring should be controlled, willing, adaptable and trained to submit to examination.

Disqualifications:
Any dog or bitch under 26 inches.
Nose other than black.
Undershot or overshot bite.
Any color other than black.

Approved: June 11, 2001
Effective: September 1, 2001

BLACK RUSSIAN TERRIER

HOW TO SELECT A PUPPY

Before deciding that you will begin your search for a Black Russian Terrier puppy, it is essential that you are absolutely certain that this is the most suitable breed for you, your family and your lifestyle. You should have carefully researched the breed prior to reaching the important decision that a Blackie should join you and your family in its daily life. This is a large-breed dog that requires the right kind of ownership...not a commitment to be taken lightly!

As important as researching the breed is finding a reputable breeder. Breed clubs, like the Black Russian Terrier Club of America, are able to supply names of breeders who are affiliated with the club and, thus, follow a strict code of ethics in their breeding programs. Dog shows are another good source of information. Potential owners are encouraged to attend dog shows (or trials) to see the Black Russian Terriers in action, to meet the owners and handlers firsthand and to get an idea of what Black Russian Terriers look

ARE YOU PREPARED?

Unfortunately, when a puppy is bought by someone who does not take into consideration the time and attention that dog ownership requires, it is the puppy who suffers when he is either abandoned or placed in a shelter by a frustrated owner. So all of the "homework" you do in preparation for your pup's arrival will benefit you both. The more informed you are, the more you will know what to expect and the better equipped you will be to handle the ups and downs of raising a puppy. Hopefully, everyone in the household is willing to do his part in raising and caring for the pup. The anticipation of owning a dog often brings a lot of promises from excited family members: "I will walk him every day," "I will feed him," "I will housebreak him," etc., but these things take time and effort, and promises can easily be forgotten once the novelty of the new pet has worn off.

like outside a photographer's lens. Provided you approach the handlers when they are not busy with the dogs, most are more than willing to answer questions, recommend breeders and give advice.

Once you are sure about your decision, you must also decide about your intentions for your dog: do you want a Blackie purely as a pet and family companion, or do you have aspirations to show your dog? If you live in a country where the breed is worked, that may be your prime interest. Your main reason for wishing to own the Black Russian should be made clear to the breeder when you make your initial inquiries, for you will need to take the breeder's advice as to which available puppy shows the most promise for your endeavors. If looking for a pet, you should discuss your family situation with the breeder and take his advice as to which puppy is likely to suit you best.

Litters of Black Russian Terriers are hard to come by, so you will most likely have to be prepared to wait. This means you will need to ask breeders about what litters are planned and how likely it is that you will be able to purchase a puppy. Many breeders have waiting lists, and sometimes prospective owners have to wait more than a year for a puppy. Litter size, on the aver-

INHERIT THE MIND
In order to know whether or not a puppy will fit into your lifestyle, you need to assess his personality. A good way to do this is to interact with his parents. Your pup inherits not only his appearance but also his personality and temperament from the sire and dam. The dam plays a big role in raising the litter, contributing to each pup's future personality and stability.

age, is roughly five or six puppies, but litter size can vary.

It is essential for you to do plenty of "homework" on the Black Russian breed so that you know as much as possible before taking that final step. Remember that the dog you select should remain with you for the duration of his life, which is generally upwards of ten years, so making the right decision from the outset

PUPPY PERSONALITY

When a litter becomes available to you, choosing the best pup for you will not be an easy task! Sound temperament is of utmost importance, but each pup has his own personality and some may be better suited to you than others. A feisty, independent pup will do well in a home with older children and adults, while quiet, shy puppies will thrive in a home with minimal noise and distractions. Your breeder knows the pups best and should be able to guide you in the right direction.

is of utmost importance. No dog should be moved from one home to another simply because the owners were thoughtless enough not to have done sufficient research before selecting the breed. It is always important to remember that, when looking for a puppy, a good breeder will be assessing you as a prospective new owner just as carefully as you are selecting the breeder.

You may have a preference between a male or a female pup. In the Blackie, there are some differences that may affect your decision. The most basic difference is that dogs generally are larger than bitches, but there are some personality differences as well. For example, males tend to challenge for position of "top dog" in the home and "test" their owners to see how much they can get away with. Females tend to be more affectionate toward their owners and more willing to accept their owners as dominant. Females also can be more wary of strangers; thus, males are often easier to socialize.

When an opportunity arises for you to visit a suitable litter, usually when the pups are five to six weeks old, watch the puppies interact together. You will find that different puppies have different personalities, and some will be more boisterous and extroverted than others. Although you will need to use your own judgment as to which puppy is most likely to fit in with your own lifestyle, and by this point you should have definite ideas about what you're looking for in a puppy, you will also be guided by the breeder's judgment and knowledge if you have chosen your breeder wisely. Breeders allow the pups to leave for their new homes between eight and ten weeks of age, no earlier.

Puppies almost invariably look enchanting, but you must select one that has been raised in a caring environment in which all of the puppies have received the necessary attention and affection, and have been well looked after. The puppy you select should look well fed, but not pot-bellied, as this might indicate worms. The eyes should look bright and clear, without discharge. The nose should be moist, an indication of good health, but should never be runny. It goes without saying that there should be no evidence of loose motions or parasites. The puppy you choose should also have a healthy-looking coat, an important indication of good health internally. Tails are docked and dewclaws removed when the pups are just a few days old.

Something else to consider is whether or not to take out veterinary insurance. Vet's bills can mount up, and you must always be certain that sufficient funds

TEMPERAMENT COUNTS
Your selection of a good puppy can be determined by your needs. A show potential or a good pet? It is your choice. Every puppy, however, should be of good temperament. Although show-quality puppies are bred and raised with emphasis on physical conformation, responsible breeders strive for equally good temperament. Do not buy from a breeder who concentrates solely on physical beauty at the expense of personality.

are available to give your dog any veterinary attention that may be needed. There are many different types of policies available, some extensive ones covering routine care like vaccinations and flea control, while others cover only major diseases and surgeries.

COMMITMENT OF OWNERSHIP
You have chosen the Black Russian Terrier as your ideal breed, which means that you

With puppy ownership comes the responsibility of training and molding your pup into a polite canine citizen.

have decided which characteristics you want in a dog and what type of dog will best fit into your family and lifestyle. If you have selected a breeder, you have gone a step further—you have done your research and found a responsible, conscientious person who breeds quality Black Russian Terriers and who should be a reliable source of help as you and your puppy adjust to life together. If you have observed a litter in action, you have obtained a firsthand look at the dynamics of a puppy "pack" and, thus, you have learned about each pup's individual personality—perhaps you have even found one that particularly appeals to you.

However, even if you have not yet found the Black Russian Terrier puppy of your dreams, observing pups will help you learn to recognize certain behavior and to determine what a pup's behavior indicates about his temperament. You will be

All puppies are cute and appealing, and a good breeder ensures that his pups radiate health and soundness from the inside out.

A HEALTHY PUP
You should not even think about buying a puppy that looks sick, undernourished, overly frightened or nervous. Sometimes a timid puppy will warm up to you after a 30-minute "let's-get-acquainted" session.

able to pick out which pups are the leaders, which ones are less outgoing, which ones are confident, shy, playful, friendly, aggressive, etc. Equally as important, you will learn to recognize what a healthy pup should look and act like. All of these things will help you in your search, and when you find the Black Russian Terrier that was meant for you, you will know it!

Researching your breed, selecting a responsible breeder and observing as many pups as possible are all important steps on the way to dog ownership. It may seem like a lot of effort…and you have not even taken the pup home yet! Remember, though, you cannot be too careful when it comes to deciding on the type of dog you want and finding out about your prospective pup's background. Buying a puppy is not—or *should* not be—just another whimsical purchase. This is one instance in which you actually do get to choose your own family! You may be thinking that buying a puppy should be fun—it should not be so serious and so much work. Keep in mind that your puppy is not a cuddly stuffed toy or decorative lawn ornament; rather, he is a living creature that will become a real member of your family. You will come to realize that, while buying a puppy is a pleasurable and exciting endeavor, it is not something to be taken lightly. Relax...the fun will start when the pup comes home!

Always keep in mind that a puppy is nothing more than a baby in a furry disguise...a baby who is virtually helpless in a human world and who trusts his owner for fulfillment of his basic needs for survival. In addition to food, water and shelter, your pup needs care, protection, guidance and love. If you are not prepared to commit to this, then you are not prepared to own a dog.

YOUR SCHEDULE . . .
If you lead an erratic, unpredictable life, with daily or weekly changes in your work requirements, consider the problems of owning a puppy. The new puppy has to be fed regularly, socialized (loved, petted, handled, introduced to other people) and, most importantly, allowed to go outdoors for housebreaking. As the dog gets older, he can become more tolerant of deviations in his feeding and relief schedule.

The BRT has a lot of growing to do before he reaches his adult size.

"Wait a minute," you say. "How hard could this be? All of my neighbors own dogs and they seem to be doing just fine. Why should I have to worry about all of this?" Well, you should not worry about it; in fact, you will probably find that once your Black Russian Terrier pup gets used to his new home, he will fall into his place in the family quite naturally. However, it never hurts to emphasize the commitment of dog ownership. With some time and patience, it is really not too difficult to raise a curious and exuberant Blackie pup to be a well-adjusted and well-mannered adult dog—a dog that could be your most loyal friend.

PREPARING PUPPY'S PLACE IN YOUR HOME

Researching your breed and finding a breeder are only two aspects of the "homework" you will have to do before taking your Black Russian Terrier puppy home. You will also have to prepare your home and family for the new addition. Much as you would prepare a nursery for a newborn baby, you will need to designate a place in your home that will be the puppy's own. How you prepare your home will depend on how much freedom the dog will be allowed. Whatever you decide, you must ensure that he has a place that he can "call his own."

When you take your new puppy into your home, you are bringing him into what will become his home as well. Obviously, you did not buy a puppy with the intentions of catering to his every whim and allowing him to "rule the roost," but in order for a puppy to grow into a stable, well-adjusted dog, he has to feel comfortable in his surroundings. Remember, he is leaving the warmth and security of his mother and littermates, as well as the familiarity of the only place he has ever known, so it is important to make his transition as easy as possible. By preparing

PEDIGREE VS. REGISTRATION CERTIFICATE

Too often new owners are confused between these two important documents. Your puppy's pedigree, essentially a family tree, is a written record of a dog's genealogy of three generations or more. The pedigree will show you the names as well as performance titles of all dogs in your pup's background. Your breeder must provide you with a registration application, with his part properly filled out. You must complete the application and send it to the AKC with the proper fee. Every puppy must come from a litter that has been AKC-registered by the breeder, born in the USA and from a sire and dam that are also registered with the AKC.

The seller must provide you with complete records to identify the puppy. The AKC requires that the seller provide the buyer with the following: breed; sex, color and markings; date of birth; litter number (when available); names and registration numbers of the parents; breeder's name; and date sold or delivered.

a place in your home for the puppy, you are making him feel as welcome as possible in a strange new place. It should not take him long to get used to it, but the sudden shock of being transplanted is somewhat traumatic for a young pup. Imagine how a small child would feel in the same situation—that is how your puppy must be feeling. It is up to you to reassure him and to let him know, "Little guy, you are going to like it here!"

WHAT YOU SHOULD BUY

CRATE

To someone unfamiliar with the use of crates in dog training, it may seem like punishment to shut a dog in a crate, but this is not the case at all. More and more breeders and trainers are recommending crates as preferred tools for pet puppies as well as show puppies. Crates are not cruel—crates have many humane and highly effective uses in dog care and training. For example, crate training is a popular and very successful housebreaking method. A crate can keep your dog safe during travel and, perhaps most importantly, a crate provides your dog with a place of his own in your home. It serves as a "doggie bedroom" of sorts— your Black Russian Terrier can curl up in his crate when he wants to sleep or when he just needs a break. Many dogs sleep in their crates overnight. With soft bedding and his favorite toy, a crate becomes a cozy pseudo-den for your dog. Like his ancestors, he too will seek out the comfort and retreat of a den—you just happen to be providing him with something a little more luxurious than what his early ancestors enjoyed.

As far as purchasing a crate, the type that you buy is up to

At nine weeks of age, this pup's first concern is what to get his teeth into next!

PHOTO COURTESY OF DOSKOCIL

Puppies do not stay puppies forever—in fact, sometimes it seems as if they grow right before your eyes. A small crate may be fine for a very young Black Russian Terrier pup, but it will not do him much good for long! Unless you have the money and the inclination to buy a new crate every time your pup has a growth spurt, it is better to get one that will accommodate your dog both as a pup and at full size. With the Blackie, a giant-sized crate will be necessary.

BEDDING

A soft crate pad or a blanket can be used to line the crate to make it comfortable for the dog. This will take the place of the leaves, twigs, etc., that the pup would use in the wild to make a den; the pup can make his own "burrow" in the crate. Although your pup is far removed from his den-making ancestors, the denning instinct is still a part of his genetic makeup.

Also, until you take your pup home, he has been sleeping amid

you. It will most likely be one of the two most popular types: wire or fiberglass. There are advantages and disadvantages to each type. For example, a wire crate is more open, allowing the air to flow through and affording the dog a view of what is going on around him; a wire crate is good for use in the home. A fiberglass crate is sturdier and is the preferred crate for travel, but a wire crate can double as a travel crate.

The size of the crate is another thing to consider.

GROWTH SPURT
The general weight for a bitch puppy at 2 months is 15–20 lb, and at 10 months she weighs 75–88 lb. A 2-month-old dog usually weighs 18–22 lb, and at 10 months is likely to be 88–99 lb.

Partitions, like gates designed for use in homes with toddlers, can be used to safely confine your puppy in a designated area of your home.

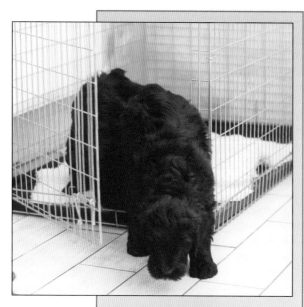

the warmth of his mother and littermates, and while a blanket is not the same as a warm, breathing body, it still provides heat and something with which to snuggle. You will want to wash your pup's bedding frequently in case he has a toileting accident in his crate, and replace or remove any blanket or padding that becomes ragged and starts to fall apart.

Toys

Toys are a must for dogs of all ages, especially for curious playful pups. Puppies are the "children" of the dog world, and what child does not love toys? Chew

CRATE-TRAINING TIPS

During crate training, you should partition off the section of the crate in which the pup stays. If he is given too big an area, this will hinder your training efforts. Crate training is based on the fact that a dog does not like to soil his sleeping quarters, so it is ineffective to keep a pup in an area that is so big that he can eliminate in one end and get far enough away from it to sleep. Also, you want to make the crate den-like for the pup. Blankets and a favorite toy will make the crate cozy for the small pup; as he grows, you may want to evict some of his "roommates" to make more room. It will take some coaxing at first, but be patient. Given some time to get used to it, your pup will adapt to his new home-within-a-home quite nicely.

Don't think that a lack of toys will stop a pup from chewing. If you don't provide him with safe chews, he will sink his teeth into whatever he can find.

toys provide enjoyment for both dog and owner—your dog will enjoy playing with his favorite toys, while you will enjoy the fact that they distract him from chewing on your expensive shoes and leather sofa. Puppies love to chew; in fact, chewing is a physical need for pups as they are teething, and everything looks appetizing! The full range of your possessions—from old dish rag to Oriental carpet—are fair game in the eyes of a teething pup. Puppies are not all that discerning when it comes to finding something literally to "sink their teeth into"—everything tastes great!

TOYS, TOYS, TOYS!

With a big variety of dog toys available, and so many that look like they would be a lot of fun for a dog, be careful in your selection. It is amazing what a set of puppy teeth can do to an innocent-looking toy, so, obviously, safety is a major consideration. Be sure to choose the most durable products that you can find. Hard nylon bones and toys are a safe bet, and many of them are offered in different scents and flavors that will be sure to capture your dog's attention. It is always fun to play a game of fetch with your dog, and there are balls and flying discs that are specially made to withstand dog teeth.

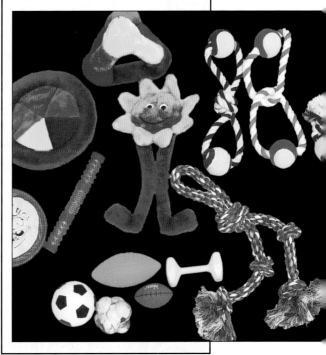

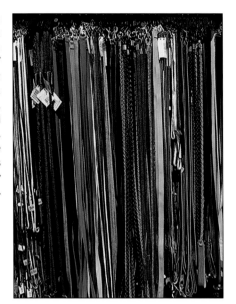

Your local pet shop should stock a wide assortment of leashes. Start your puppy on a lightweight leash, keeping in mind that, as he grows, he will become stronger and thus require a stronger leash.

Black Russian Terriers are not particularly aggressive chewers, but will they will enjoy toys. The toys you offer should be completely safe, with no removable parts. The BRT needs highly durable toys and chews. Keep the breed's large size in mind and provide appropriately sized toys. Balls should never be so small that they might be swallowed accidentally.

Breeders advise owners to resist stuffed toys, because they can become de-stuffed in no time. The overly excited pup may ingest the stuffing, which is neither nutritious nor digestible. Similarly, squeaky toys are quite popular, but must be avoided for the Black Russian Terrier. Perhaps a squeaky toy can be used as an aid in training, but not for free play. If a pup "disembowels" one of these, the small plastic squeaker inside can be dangerous if swallowed. Monitor the condition of all your pup's toys carefully and get rid of any that have been chewed to the point of becoming potentially dangerous.

Be careful of natural bones, which have a tendency to splinter into sharp, dangerous pieces. Also be careful of rawhide, which can turn into pieces that are easy to swallow and become a mushy mess on your carpet.

Leash

A nylon leash is probably the best option, as it is the most resistant to puppy teeth should your pup take a liking to chewing on his leash. Of course, this is a habit that should be nipped in the bud, but, if your pup likes to chew on his leash, he has a very slim chance of being able to chew through the strong nylon. Nylon leashes are also lightweight, which is good for a young Black Russian Terrier who is just getting used to the idea of walking on a leash. For everyday walking and safety purposes, the nylon leash is a good choice.

As your pup grows up, and gets larger and stronger, you will need to purchase a stronger leash. Of course, there are leashes designed for training

CHOOSE AN APPROPRIATE COLLAR

The BUCKLE COLLAR is the standard collar used for everyday purposes. Be sure that you adjust the buckle on growing puppies. Check it every day. It can become too tight overnight! These collars can be made of leather or nylon. Attach your dog's identification tags to this collar.

The CHOKE COLLAR is designed for training. It is constructed of highly polished steel so that it slides easily through the stainless steel loop. The idea is that the dog controls the pressure around his neck and he will stop pulling if the collar becomes uncomfortable. It is used during training sessions only and *never* left on a dog.

The HALTER is for a trained dog that has to be restrained to prevent running away, chasing a cat and the like. Considered the most humane of all collars, it is frequently used on smaller dogs on which collars are not comfortable.

Purchase appropriately sized, sturdy and easily cleaned bowls for your Black Russian's food and water.

PHOTO COURTESY OF MIKKI PET PRODUCTS.

purposes and specially made harnesses worn by working dogs, but these are not necessary for routine walks.

COLLAR

Your pup should get used to wearing a collar all the time since you will want to attach his ID tags to it; plus, you have to attach the leash to something! A lightweight nylon collar is a good choice. Make certain that the collar fits snugly enough so that the pup cannot wriggle out of it, but is loose enough so that it will not be uncomfortably tight around the pup's neck. You should be able to fit a finger between the pup's neck and the collar. It may take some time for your pup to get used to wearing the collar, but soon he will not even notice that it is there. The choke collar is made for training, but should only be used by an owner who has been instructed in its proper use.

FOOD AND WATER BOWLS

Your pup will need two bowls, one for food and one for water. You may want two sets of bowls, one for indoors and one for outdoors, depending on where the dog will be fed and where he will be spending time. Stainless steel or sturdy plastic bowls are popular choices. Plastic bowls are more chewable, but dogs tend not to chew on the steel variety,

which can be sterilized. It is important to buy sturdy bowls since anything is in danger of being chewed by puppy teeth and you do not want your dog to be constantly chewing apart his bowl (for his safety and for your wallet!).

As a preventative measure against bloat/gastric torsion, the potentially deadly condition that affects deep-chested breeds like the Black Russian, you should purchase stands on which to elevate your dog's bowls. By elevating the bowls so that the dog doesn't have to crane his neck to eat, there is less risk of his swallowing air, one of the causes of bloat.

CLEANING SUPPLIES

Until a pup is housebroken, you will be doing a lot of cleaning. "Accidents" will occur, which is acceptable in the beginning stages of toilet training because the puppy does not know any better. All you can do is be prepared to clean up any accidents as soon as they happen. Old towels, paper towels, newspapers and a safe disinfectant are good to have on hand.

Feeding and offering water to a Black Russian Terrier is best done in elevated bowls. By bringing the bowls closer to his level, you are creating a more comfortable feeding position, thus aiding digestion and reducing the risk of his swallowing air and developing the potentially deadly bloat.

BEYOND THE BASICS

The items previously discussed are the bare necessities. You will find out what else you need as you go along—grooming supplies, flea/tick protection, baby gates to partition a room, etc. These things will vary depending on your situation, but it is important that right away you have everything you need to feed and make your Black Russian Terrier comfortable in his first few days at home.

MENTAL AND DENTAL

Toys not only help your Blackie get the physical and mental stimulation he needs but also provide a great way to keep his teeth clean. Hard rubber or nylon toys, especially those constructed with grooves, are designed to scrape away plaque, preventing bad breath and gum infection.

PUPPY-PROOFING YOUR HOME

Aside from making sure that your Black Russian Terrier will be comfortable in your home, you also have to make sure that your home is safe for your Black Russian Terrier. This means taking precautions that your pup will not get into anything he should not get into and that there is nothing within his reach that may harm him should he sniff it, chew it, inspect it, etc. This probably seems obvious since, while you are primarily concerned with your pup's safety, at the same time you do not want your belongings to be ruined. Breakables should be placed out of reach if your dog is to have full run of the house. If he is to be limited to certain places within the house, keep any potentially dangerous items in the "off-limits" areas.

An electrical cord can pose a danger should the puppy decide to taste it—and who is going to convince a pup that it would not make a great chew toy? Cords and wires should be fastened tightly against the wall and kept from puppy teeth. If your dog is going to spend time in a crate, make sure that there is nothing near his crate that he can reach if he sticks his curious little nose or paws through the openings. Just as you would with a child, keep all household cleaners and chemicals where the pup cannot reach them. Antifreeze is particiularly deadly to dogs.

It is also important to make sure that the outside of your home is safe. Of course, your puppy should never be unsupervised, but a pup let loose in the yard will want to run and explore, and he should be granted that freedom. Do not let a fence give you a false sense of security; you would be surprised at how crafty (and persistent) a dog can be in figuring out how to dig under and squeeze his way through small holes, or to jump or climb over a fence. Whether or not a Blackie is an "escape artist" will vary among each individual dog, but they are certainly capable of jumping and can be diggers. The remedy is to make the fence well embedded into the ground (at least a foot deep) and high enough so that it really is impossible for your dog to get over it (at least 6 feet should suffice). Be sure to secure any gaps in the fence. Check the fence periodically to ensure that it is in good shape and make repairs as needed; a very determined pup may return to the same spot to "work on it" until he is able to get through.

FIRST TRIP TO THE VET

You have selected your puppy, and your home and family are ready. Now all you have to do is

TOXIC PLANTS
Many plants can be toxic to dogs. If you see your dog carrying a piece of vegetation in his mouth, approach him in a quiet, disinterested manner, avoid eye contact, pet him and gradually remove the plant from his mouth. Alternatively, offer him a treat and maybe he'll drop the plant on his own accord. Be sure no toxic plants are growing in your own yard or kept in your home.

collect your Black Russian Terrier from the breeder and the fun begins, right? Well...not so fast. Something else you need to plan is your pup's first trip to the veterinarian. Perhaps the breeder can recommend someone in the area with experience in Black Russians or similar large-breed dogs, or maybe you know some other dog owners who can suggest a good vet. Either way, you should have an appointment arranged for your pup before you pick him up.

The pup's first visit will consist of an overall examination to make sure that the pup does not have any problems that are not apparent to you. The veterinarian will also set up a schedule for the pup's vaccinations; the breeder will inform you of which ones the pup has already received and the vet can continue from there.

INTRODUCTION TO THE FAMILY

Everyone in the house will be excited about the puppy's coming home and will want to pet him and play with him, but it is best to make the introduction low-key

It's a big world to a small pup, although the BRT grows into it sooner than you know it. Allow for an adjustment period and help your pup become comfortable in his new home.

THE COCOA WARS
Chocolate contains the chemical thebromine, which is poisonous to dogs, although "chocolates" especially made for dogs are safe (as they don't actually contain chocolate) but not recommended. Any item that encourages your dog to enjoy the taste of cocoa should be discouraged. You should also exercise caution when using mulch in your garden. This frequently contains cocoa hulls, and dogs have been known to die from eating the mulch.

so as not to overwhelm the puppy. He is apprehensive already. It is the first time he has been separated from his mother and the breeder, and the ride to your home is likely to be the first time he has been in a car. The last thing you want to do is smother him, as this will only frighten him further. This is not to say that human contact is not extremely necessary at this stage, because this is the time when a connection between the pup and his human family is formed. Gentle petting and soothing words should help console him, as well as just putting him down and letting him explore on his own (under your watchful eye, of course).

The pup may approach the family members or may busy himself with exploring for a while. Gradually, each person should spend some time with the pup, one at a time, crouching down to get as close to the pup's level as possible, letting him sniff each person's hands and petting him gently. He definitely needs human attention and he needs to be touched—this is how to form an immediate bond. Just remember that the pup is experiencing many things for the first time, at the same time. There are new people, new noises, new smells and new things to investigate, so be gentle, be affectionate and be as comforting as you can be.

PUP'S FIRST NIGHT HOME

You have traveled home with your new charge safely in his crate. He's been to the vet for a thorough check-up; he's been weighed, his papers have been examined and perhaps he's even been vaccinated and wormed as well. He's met (and licked!) the whole family, including the excited children and the less-than-happy cat. He's explored his area, his new bed, the yard and anywhere else he's been permitted. He's eaten his first meal at home and relieved himself in the proper place. He's heard lots of new sounds, smelled new friends and seen more of the outside world than ever before...and that was just the first day! He's worn out and is ready for bed...or so you think!

MANNERS MATTER

During the socialization process, a puppy should meet people, experience different environments and definitely be exposed to other canines. Through playing and interacting with other dogs, your puppy will learn lessons, ranging from controlling the pressure of his jaws by biting his littermates to the inner-workings of the canine pack that he will apply to his human relationships for the rest of his life. That is why removing a puppy from the litter too early (before eight weeks) can be detrimental to the pup's development.

It's puppy's first night home and you are ready to say "Good night." Keep in mind that this is his first night ever to be sleeping alone. His dam and littermates are no longer at paw's length and

SOCIALIZATION PERIOD

The socialization period for puppies is from age 8 to 16 weeks. This is the time when puppies need to leave their birth family and take up residence with their new owners, where they will meet many new people, other pets, etc. Failure to be adequately socialized can cause the dog to grow up fearing others and being shy and unfriendly due to a lack of self-confidence.

"Patient" and "prepared" are two other "p" words associated with house-breaking: be patient with the puppy and be prepared to clean up!

he's a bit scared, cold and lonely. Be reassuring to your new family member, but this is not the time to spoil him and give in to his inevitable whining.

Puppies whine. They whine to let others know where they are and hopefully to get company out of it. Place your pup in his new bed or crate in his designated area and close the crate door. Mercifully, he may fall asleep without a peep. When the

inevitable occurs, however, ignore the whining—he is fine. Be strong and keep his interest in mind. Do not allow yourself to feel guilty and visit the pup. He will fall asleep eventually.

Many breeders recommend placing a piece of bedding from the pup's former home in his new bed so that he recognizes and is comforted by the scent of his littermates. Others still advise placing a hot-water bottle in the bed for warmth. The latter may be a good idea provided the pup doesn't attempt to suckle—he'll get good and wet, and may not fall asleep so fast.

Puppy's first night can be somewhat stressful for both the pup and his new family. Remember that you are setting the tone of nighttime at your house. Unless you want to play with your pup every night at 10 p.m., midnight and 2 a.m., don't initiate the habit. Your family will thank you, and eventually so will your pup!

PREVENTING PUPPY PROBLEMS

SOCIALIZATION

Now that you have done all of the preparatory work and have helped your pup get accustomed to his new home and family, it is about time for you to have some fun! Socializing your Black Russian Terrier pup gives you the

opportunity to show off your new friend—likely you will be the only one in the neighborhood with this intriguing rare breed—and your pup gets to reap the benefits of being an adorable furry creature that people will want to pet and, in general, think is absolutely precious!

Besides getting to know his new family, your puppy should be exposed to other people, animals and situations. This will help him become well adjusted as he grows up and less prone to being timid or fearful of the new things he will encounter. Of course, he must not come into close contact with dogs you don't know well until his course of injections is fully complete, but it is important to introduce him to other dogs. Male Black Russians especially can be dominant, and this can cause them to be dog-aggressive if not socialized. However, in general, BRTs are not the first to be the aggressors.

Your pup's socialization began with the breeder, but now it is your responsibility to continue it. The socialization he receives until the age of 12 weeks is the most critical, as this is the time when he forms his impressions of the outside world. Be especially careful during the eight-to-ten-week-old period, also known as the fear period. If you have your Blackie pup at this

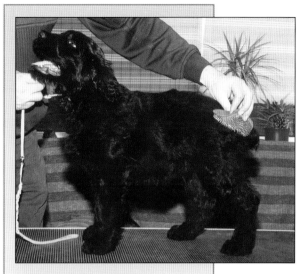

PUP MEETS WORLD
Thorough socialization includes not only meeting new people but also being introduced to new experiences such as riding in the car, having his coat brushed, hearing the television, walking in a crowd—the list is endless. The more your pup experiences, and the more positive the experiences are, the less of a shock and the less frightening it will be for your pup to encounter new things.

age, remember that the interaction he receives during this time should be gentle and reassuring. Lack of socialization, and/or negative experiences during the socialization period, can manifest itself in fear and aggression as the dog grows up. Your puppy needs lots of positive interaction, which of course includes human contact, affection, handling and

and pups most often make great companions. However, sometimes an excited child can unintentionally handle a pup too roughly, or an overzealous pup can playfully nip a little too hard. You want to make socialization experiences positive ones. What a pup learns during this very formative stage will affect his attitude toward future encounters. You want your dog to be comfortable around everyone. A pup that has a bad experience with a child may grow up to be a dog that is shy around or aggressive toward children.

CONSISTENCY IN TRAINING

Dogs, being pack animals, naturally need a leader, or else they

This small toy is no match for the Blackie's large teeth and strong jaws. The toys offered to your BRT should be those made for large dogs, and the strongest, most durable available.

exposure to other animals.

Once your pup has received his necessary vaccinations, feel free to take him out and about (on his leash, of course). Walk him around the neighborhood, take him on your daily errands, let people pet him, let him meet other dogs and pets, etc. Puppies do not have to try to make friends; there will be no shortage of people who will want to introduce themselves. Just make sure that you carefully supervise each meeting. If the neighborhood children want to say hello, for example, that is great—children

PLAY'S THE THING

Teaching the puppy to play with his toys in running and fetching games is an ideal way to help the puppy develop muscle, learn motor skills and bond with you, his owner and master. He also needs to learn how to inhibit his bite reflex and never to use his teeth on people, forbidden objects and other animals in play. Whenever you play with your puppy, you make the rules. This becomes an important message to your puppy in teaching him that you are the pack leader and control everything he does in life. Once your dog accepts you as his leader, your relationship with him will be cemented for life.

try to establish dominance in their packs. When you welcome a dog into your family, the choice of who becomes the leader and who becomes the "pack" is entirely up to you! Your pup's intuitive quest for dominance, coupled with the fact that it is nearly impossible to look at an adorable Black Russian Terrier pup with his "puppy-dog" eyes and not cave in, give the pup almost an unfair advantage in getting the upper hand! A pup will definitely test the waters to see what he can and cannot do.

Do not give in to those pleading eyes—stand your ground when it comes to disciplining the pup and make sure that all family members do the same. It will only confuse the pup if Mother tells him to get off the sofa when he is used to sitting up there with Father to watch the nightly news.

Avoid discrepancies by having all members of the household decide on the rules before the pup even comes home…and be consistent in enforcing them! Early training shapes the dog's personality, so you cannot be unclear in what you expect.

COMMON PUPPY PROBLEMS
The best way to prevent puppy problems is to be proactive in stopping an undesirable behavior as soon as it starts. The old saying "You can't teach an old dog new tricks" does not necessarily hold true, but it *is* true that it is much easier to discourage bad behavior in a young developing pup than to wait until the pup's bad behavior becomes the adult dog's bad habit. There are some problems that are especially prevalent in puppies as they develop.

The loyal Black Russian isn't afraid to show his owner how he feels!

I'M HOME!
Dogs left alone for varying lengths of time may often react wildly when their owners return. Sometimes they run, jump, bite, chew, tear things apart, wet themselves, gobble their food or behave in very undisciplined ways. If your dog behaves in this manner upon your return home, allow him to calm down before greeting him or he will consider your attention as a reward for his antics.

NIPPING
As puppies start to teethe, they feel the need to sink their teeth into anything available...unfortunately, that usually includes your fingers, arms, hair and toes. You may find this behavior cute for the first five seconds...until you feel just how sharp those puppy teeth are. Nipping is something you want to discourage immediately and consistently with a firm "No!" (or whatever number of firm "Nos" it takes for him to understand that you mean business). Then, replace your finger with an appropriate chew toy. While this behavior is merely annoying when the dog is young, it can become dangerous as your Black Russian Terrier's adult teeth grow in and his jaws develop, and he continues to think it is okay to gnaw on human appendages. Your Black Russian Terrier does not mean any harm with a friendly nip, but he also does not know the strength of his powerful jaws.

CRYING/WHINING
Your pup will often cry, whine, whimper, howl or make some type of commotion when he is left alone. This is basically his way of calling out for attention to make sure that you know he is there and that you have not forgotten about him. Your puppy feels insecure when he is left

alone, when you are out of the house and he is in his crate or when you are in another part of the house and he cannot see you. The noise he is making is an expression of the anxiety he feels at being alone, so he needs to be taught that being alone is okay. You are not actually training the dog to stop making noise; rather, you are training him to feel comfortable when he is alone and thus removing the need for him to make the noise.

This is where the crate with cozy bedding and a toy comes in handy. You want to know that your pup is safe when you are not there to supervise, and you know that he will be safe in his crate rather than roaming freely about the house. In order for the pup to stay in his crate without making a fuss, he first needs to be comfortable in his crate. On that note, it is extremely important that the crate is never used as a form of punishment; this will cause the pup to view the crate as a negative place, rather than as a place of his own for safety and retreat.

Accustom the pup to the crate in short, gradually increasing time intervals in which you put him in the crate, maybe with a treat, and stay in the room with him. If he cries or makes a fuss, do not go to him, but stay in his sight. Gradually he will realize that staying in his crate is just fine without your help, and it will not be so traumatic for him when you are not around. You may want to leave the radio on softly when you leave the house; the sound of human voices may be comforting to him.

CHEWING TIPS

Chewing goes hand in hand with nipping in the sense that a teething puppy is always looking for a way to soothe his aching gums. In this case, instead of chewing on you, he may have taken a liking to your favorite shoe or something else that he should not be chewing. Again, realize that this is a normal canine behavior that does not need to be discouraged, only redirected. Your pup just needs to be taught what is acceptable to chew on and what is off-limits. Consistently tell him "No!" when you catch him chewing on something forbidden and give him a chew toy.

Conversely, praise him when you catch him chewing on something appropriate. In this way, you are discouraging the inappropriate behavior and reinforcing the desired behavior. The puppy's chewing should stop after his adult teeth have come in, but an adult dog continues to chew for various reasons—perhaps because he is bored, needs to relieve tension or just likes to chew. That is why it is important to redirect his chewing when he is still young.

BLACK RUSSIAN TERRIER

FEEDING CONSIDERATIONS

A Black Russian Terrier should be fed sensibly on a high-quality diet. With so many first-rate canine food products now available, it will be very much a matter of personal preference, along with advice from the breeder and vet, as to which one is chosen. A carefully selected breeder will be able to give good advice in this regard, as he will have experience and knowledge of which foods have been good for his own dogs at the different stages of life.

Supplements to a nutritionally complete food should be avoided unless advised by the breeder or vet. Please take care that you do not allow your Blackie to put on excess weight, for an overweight dog is more prone to health problems than one that is of correct weight for his size. Feeding any dog too many tidbits between meals will run the risk of having an unhealthy, overweight dog. Carrots are an excellent treat for a dog; they will not cause the dog put on weight and will help to keep teeth clean.

When you take your puppy home, the breeder should provide you with a diet sheet that gives details of exactly how your puppy has been fed. Of course, you will be at liberty to change the food, together with the frequency and timing of meals, as the youngster reaches adulthood, but changes should be done gradually. It is never

STORING DOG FOOD

You must store your dry dog food carefully. Open packages of dog food quickly lose their vitamin value, usually within 90 days of being opened. Mold spores and vermin could also contaminate the food.

wise to change suddenly from one diet to another, for this is likely to result in an upset stomach.

Some owners prefer to feed fresh food rather than commercial diets. Brown rice is an excellent nutritional source and can be easily digested and assimilated into the system. Brown rice mixed with lamb is something often recommended for dogs that suffer from allergies. It is also worth bearing in mind that if you have a "finicky eater," although you have to be very careful not to unbalance an otherwise balanced complete commerical food, sometimes a little added fresh meat, or even just gravy or stock, will gain a dog's interest and stimulate the appetite.

Because your Black Russian Terrier's food has a bearing on coat, health and temperament, it is essential that the most suitable diet is selected for a Black Russian Terrier of his age. It is easy for an owner to be confused, given the wide variety of foods available. Only understanding what is best for your dog will help you reach an informed choice.

Dog foods are produced in three basic types: dry, semi-moist and canned. Dry foods are useful for the cost-conscious, for overall they tend to be less expensive than semi-moist or canned foods. Dry foods also contain the least fat and the most preservatives. In general, canned foods are made up

Select your Blackie's food with care and feed proper amounts to maintain a healthy weight. The BRT should be massive, but this should not be confused with allowing your dog to be too heavy for his size.

of 60–70 % water, while semi-moist ones often contain so much sugar that they are perhaps the least preferred by owners, even though their dogs seem to like them.

When selecting your dog's diet, three stages of development must be considered: the puppy stage, the adult stage and the senior stage.

PUPPY STAGE
Puppies instinctively want to suck milk from their mother's teats; a

normal puppy will exhibit this behavior just a few moments following birth. If puppies do not attempt to suckle within the first half-hour or so, the breeder should encourage them to do so by placing them on the nipples, having selected ones with plenty of milk. This early milk supply is important in providing the essential colostrum, which protects the puppies during the first eight to ten weeks of their lives. Although a mother's milk is much better than any commercially prepared milk formula, despite there being some excellent ones available, if the puppies do not feed, the breeder will have to feed them by hand. For those with less experience, advice from a veterinarian is important so that not only the right quantity of milk is fed but also that of correct quality, fed at suitably frequent intervals, usually every two hours during the first few days of life.

Puppies should be allowed to nurse from their dam for about the first six weeks, although, starting around the third or fourth week, the breeder will begin to introduce small portions of suitable solid food. Most breeders like to introduce alternate milk and meat meals initially, building up to weaning time.

By the time the puppies are seven or a maximum of eight weeks old, they should be fully weaned and fed solely on a proprietary puppy food. Selection of the most suitable, good-quality diet at this time is essential, for a puppy's fastest growth rate is during the first year of life. Again, veterinarians and breeders should be able to offer advice in this regard.

The frequency of meals will be reduced over time, and eventually the maturing pup can be switched to an adult dog food. Some brands have a slight variation for "juniors," which may be used as a transition between the puppy food and adult food. Puppy and junior diets should be well balanced for the needs of your dog so that, except in certain circumstances, additional vitamins, minerals and proteins will not be required or recommended.

ADULT DIETS
The age at which to switch a Black Russian to an adult food can vary according to the brand of food used and the individual pup's bodily development. BRTs generally begin on adult diets by 10 to 12 months of age, but this

TEST FOR PROPER DIET
A good test for proper diet is the color, odor and firmness of your dog's stool. A healthy dog usually produces three semi-hard stools per day. The stools should have no unpleasant odor. They should be the same color from excretion to excretion.

depends very much upon the individual. This is a slow-maturing breed with much variation in size, so there's not a "one-size-fits-all" answer to the question of when to change the diet.

Again you should rely upon your veterinarian, your breeder or a dietary specialist to recommend an acceptable maintenance diet. Major dog-food manufacturers specialize in this type of food, and it is merely necessary for you to select the one best suited to your dog's needs. For example, active dogs have different requirements than sedate dogs.

SENIOR DIETS

As dogs get older, their metabolism changes. The older dog usually exercises less, moves more slowly and sleeps more. This change in lifestyle and physiological performance requires a change in diet. Since these changes take place slowly, they might not be recognizable. What is easily recognizable is weight gain. By continuing to feed your dog an adult-maintenance diet when he is slowing down metabolically, your dog will gain weight. Obesity in an older dog compounds the health problems that already accompany old age.

As your dog gets older, few of his organs function up to par. The kidneys slow down and the intestines become less efficient. These age-related factors are best

FOOD PREFERENCE
Selecting the best diet for your dog is difficult. There is no majority consensus among veterinary scientists as to the value of nutrient analysis (protein, fat, fiber, moisture, ash, cholesterol, minerals, etc.). All agree that feeding trials are what matter most, but you also have to consider the individual dog. The dog's weight, age and activity level, and what pleases his taste, all must be considered. It is probably best to take the advice of your veterinarian. Every dog's dietary requirements vary, even during the lifetime of a particular dog.

If your dog is fed a good dry food, he does not require supplements of meat or vegetables. Dogs do appreciate a little variety in their diets, so you may choose to stay with the same brand but vary the flavor. Alternatively, you may wish to add a little flavored stock to give a difference to the taste.

handled with a change in diet and a change in feeding schedule to give smaller portions that are more easily digested.

Some BRTs never change to a senior diet, but others move over from about seven or eight years of age. There is no single best diet for every older dog. While many dogs do well on light or senior diets, other dogs do better on special premium diets such as lamb and rice. Be sensitive to your senior Black Russian Terrier's diet, as this will help control other problems that may arise with your old friend.

With eating and drinking come drooling and dripping! The BRT's facial furnishings collect food and water and can be prone to matting, so extra attention should be paid to these areas.

DO DOGS HAVE TASTE BUDS?
Watching a dog "wolf" or gobble his food, seemingly without chewing, leads an owner to wonder whether his dog can taste anything. Yes, dogs have taste buds, with sensory perception of sweet, salty and sour. Puppies are born with fully mature taste buds.

WATER
Just as your dog needs proper nutrition from his food, water is an essential "nutrient" as well. Water keeps the dog's body properly hydrated and promotes normal function of the body's systems. During the housebreaking process, it is necessary to keep an eye on how much water your Black Russian Terrier is drinking, but, once he is reliably trained, he should have access to clean fresh water at all times. Keep in mind though, that it is best to limit water intake at meals, and never allow your BRT to gulp water at any time. Make certain that the dog's water bowl is clean and elevated and change the water often.

EXERCISE
The Black Russian Terrier is a large, highly active breed that needs plenty of exercise. Exercise is necessary for both his health and happiness. However, this tends to be a "one-man" breed, and may even resent being taken

out by anyone other than his owner(s).

Because this is a dog that was bred as a working animal, and because of the breed's tendency to guard, safety is of utmost importance when allowing your dog to run free. Your Black Russian Terrier must always be kept under supervision in a public place, especially if off-leash. For the dog's safety, all possible escape routes should be thoroughly checked and secured before taking

Wiping the face with a soft towel after mealtimes and water breaks will help keep the long facial hair clean.

him off the leash. Of course, your yard also needs to be safely enclosed by fencing, which should be checked at regular intervals.

Exercising your Black Russian Terrier can be enjoyable and healthy for both of you. You don't want to overdo exercise with a growing puppy, as it runs the risk of damaging his developing frame, but as the puppy gets older, brisk walks will stimulate heart rates and build muscle for both dog and owner. As the dog reaches adulthood, the speed and distance of the walks can be increased as long as they are both kept reasonable and comfortable for both of you.

Play sessions in the yard and letting the dog run free in the yard under your supervision also are sufficient forms of exercise for the

DRINK, DRANK, DRUNK— MAKE IT A DOUBLE

In both humans and dogs, as well as other living organisms, water forms the major part of nearly every body tissue. Naturally, we take water for granted, but without it, life as we know it would cease.

For dogs, water is needed to keep their bodies functioning biochemically. Additionally, water is needed to replace the water lost while panting. Unlike humans, who are able to sweat to dissipate heat, dogs must pant to cool down, thereby losing the vital water that their bodies need to regulate their body temperatures. Humans lose electrolyte-containing products and other body-fluid components through sweating; dogs do not lose anything except water.

Water is essential always, but especially so when the weather is hot or humid or when your dog is exercising or working vigorously.

Black Russian Terrier. Fetching games can be played indoors or out; these are excellent for giving your dog active play that he will enjoy. Chasing things that move comes naturally to dogs of all breeds. When your Black Russian Terrier runs after the ball or another object, praise him for picking it up and encourage him to bring it back to you for another throw. Never go to the object and pick it up yourself, or you'll soon find that you are the one retrieving the objects rather than the dog! If you choose to play games outdoors, you must have a securely fenced-in yard or have the dog attached to at least a 25-foot light line for security. You want your Black Russian Terrier to run, but not run away!

Bear in mind that an over-weight dog should never be suddenly over-exercised; instead, he should be encouraged to increase exercise slowly. Also keep in mind that you should restrict

Make your yard a safe enclosed area where your Blackie can run and play. He will get a lot of exercise on his own, but remember that the best exercise comes from activities in which owner and dog spend time together.

exercise around mealtimes, allowing the dog to rest for *at least* an hour before and after eating.

Not only is exercise essential to keep the dog's body fit, it is essential to his mental well-being. A bored dog will find something to do, which often manifests itself in some type of destructive behavior. In this sense, exercise is essential for the owner's mental well-being as well!

GROOMING

COAT MAINTENANCE AND TRIMMING
Unless you are prepared to groom your dog regularly, the Black Russian Terrier is absolutely not the breed for you. At the minimum, the dog will require everyday brushing with a slicker brush to keep the coat mat-free. Throughout the world, it is accepted that this is a trimmed breed, which means that it is effectively "sculptured" for exhibition at shows, though a BRT kept purely as a pet would probably not be trimmed so precisely. The guidelines for trimming can be modified for the pet owner's personal preference.

As this is a relatively new breed, there is still some debate among owners as to exactly how much trimming should take place, and the exact manner in which it should be done, so readers will appreciate that only general guidelines are given here.

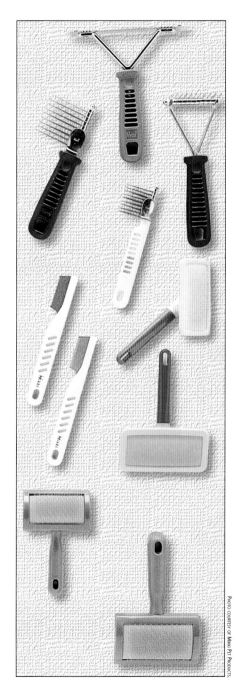

Your local pet shop probably has a complete range of brushes, combs and other grooming tools to keep your Blackie's coat in top condition.

PHOTO COURTESY OF MIKKI PET PRODUCTS.

It is important to brush out the coat and bathe the dog the day prior to trimming, or even in the morning if you plan to trim in the evening. A coat that has been freshly bathed will have less noticeable trim lines. At this time, any knots that have formed will have to be carefully removed (if the coat is very matted, detangling should be done before bathing). Always free tight knots from the skin outward, instead of the other way around, as this would only serve to tighten the mat further. Use a slicker brush to untangle any mats.

When you do start to trim, ensure that the coat is dry and always remember that you must trim in the direction of coat growth. Scissors are used to trim the mane, jacket and chest. Leg furnishings must also be trimmed carefully into shape. Certain areas on this breed are trimmed close, and in such instances clippers and thinning scissors are used. This is the method used for trimming the skull, from the fold of the ears to the tip, the neck and the front down to the bib (which is just above the point of chest), the rear of the tail and the hindquarters (to show the bend of stifle).

The edges of the ears and the anal area need scissoring to give them the "finishing touch," and scissors are also used to shape the tail tip. Usually the last job to be done is shaping of the feet, also with scissors. For this, you will probably find it best to pick up each foot, one at a time, and hold the ankle while you scissor around the edge of the toes. When you put the foot back on the table and comb it through, you will be able to make any minor corrections that are necessary, always keeping in mind that the foot should not flair out from the leg.

It is of the utmost importance for you to know beforehand what you are aiming for as the end result, so it may be a good idea to have a grooming chart or a picture of a top-winning BRT on hand for reference. It is a good idea to remove your dog from the grooming table occasionally so that you can see how different areas are

GROOMING EQUIPMENT

The BRT requires frequent grooming, so select quality equipment that will last for years of use. Here are some basics:

- Slicker brush
- Metal comb
- Scissors
- Electric clippers
- Rubber mat
- Dog shampoo
- Spray hose attachment
- Towels
- Ear cleaner
- Cotton balls
- Nail clippers
- Tooth-care products

"I'm ready!" Once trained, your BRT will know that the grooming table is his "beauty parlor," and he should look forward to his routine sessions with you.

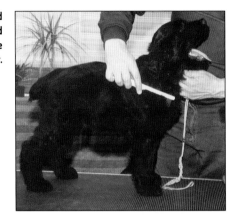

A wide-toothed comb can be used gently on the puppy coat.

A grooming glove with bristles is a useful tool, and the dog should grow to like the feel of being massaged while you brush.

After a thorough brushing, an equally thorough comb-through will ensure that the coat is tangle-free.

progressing. You will especially need to check mane and shoulder, topline and leg furnishings. Most breeders advise that the eyebrows, mustache and beard are left untouched.

Undoubtedly grooming of this kind is an art, and novice owners will improve with experience. The Black Russian Terrier's coat grows quite quickly, so you will have plenty of opportunity to practice your art!

BATHING

Dogs do not need to be bathed as often as humans, but bathing as needed is essential for healthy skin and a clean, shiny coat. Again, like most anything, if you accustom your pup to being bathed as a puppy, it will be second nature by the time he grows up. You want your dog to be at ease in the bath or else it could end up a wet, soapy, messy ordeal for both of you!

Brush your Black Russian Terrier thoroughly before wetting his coat. This will get rid of most mats and tangles, which are harder to remove when the coat is wet. Make certain that your dog has a good non-slip surface on which to stand. Begin by wetting the dog's coat, checking the water temperature to make sure that it is neither too hot nor too cold for the dog. A shower or hose attachment is necessary for thoroughly wetting and rinsing the coat.

Next, apply shampoo to the dog's coat and work it into a good lather. Wash the head last, as you do not want shampoo to drip into the dog's eyes while you are washing the rest of his body. You should use only a shampoo that is made for dogs. Do not use a product made for human hair. Work the shampoo all the way down to the skin. You can use this opportunity to check the skin for any bumps, bites or other abnormalities. Do not neglect any area of the body—get all of the hard-to-reach places.

Once the dog has been thoroughly shampooed, he requires an equally thorough rinsing. Shampoo left in the coat can be irritating to the dog's skin. Protect his eyes from the shampoo by shielding them with your hand and directing the flow of water in the opposite direction. You also should avoid getting water in the ear canal. Be prepared for your dog to shake out his coat—you might want to stand back, but make sure you have a hold on the dog to keep him from running through the house, and have a heavy towel close at hand.

EAR CLEANING

The ears should be kept clean with a cotton ball and ear cleaner made especially for dogs. Do not probe into the ear canal with a cotton swab, as this can cause injury. Excess hair will need to be

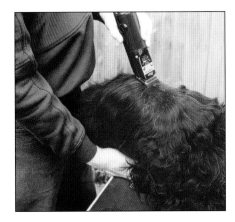

Using a clipper requires skill and practice. Learn from an experienced groomer.

The outline of the dog is enhanced by shaping with a comb and scissors.

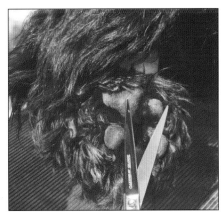

The hair between the footpads should be trimmed. If the hair grows too long, it will cause the dog discomfort as well as collect debris that can lead to matting.

Nail Clipping

Quick

Cut Line

Nail Casing

DARK-COLORED NAIL

With black or dark nails, it's best to clip only a small bit of the nail at a time or to use a file where the quick is not visible.

LIGHT-COLORED NAIL

In light-colored nails, clipping is much simpler because you can see the vein (or quick) that grows inside the nail casing.

plucked from the ear on a regular basis; this should not cause pain to the dog if you do it gently.

When cleaning and checking your Blackie's ears, be on the look-out for any signs of infection or ear-mite infestation. If your Black Russian Terrier has been shaking his head or scratching at his ears frequently, this usually indicates a problem. If the dog's ears have an unusual odor, this is a sure sign of mite infestation or infection, and a signal to have his ears checked by the veterinarian.

NAIL CLIPPING

Your Black Russian Terrier should be accustomed to having his nails trimmed at an early age since nail clipping will be part of your maintenance routine throughout his life. A dog's long nails can scratch someone unintentionally and also have a better chance of ripping and bleeding, or of causing the feet to spread. A good rule of thumb is that if you can hear your dog's nails' clicking on the floor when he walks, his nails are too long.

Before you start cutting, make sure you can identify the "quick" in each nail. The quick is a blood vessel that runs through the center of each nail and grows rather close to the end. The quick will bleed if accidentally cut, which will be quite painful for the dog as it contains nerve endings. Keep some type of clotting agent on

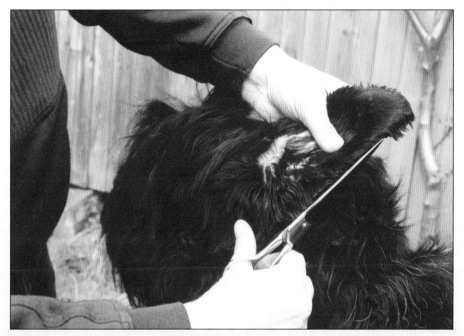

Hair on the edges of the ear should be neatened up carefully, trimming around the outline of the ear.

The outer ears should be cleaned with a soft wipe or cotton ball and an ear-cleaning liquid or powder made for dogs. *Never* enter the ear canal.

hand, such as a styptic pencil or styptic powder (the type used for shaving). This will stop the bleeding quickly when applied to the end of the cut nail. Do not panic if you cut the quick, just stop the bleeding and talk soothingly to your dog. Once he has calmed down, move on to the next nail. It is better to clip a little at a time, particularly with black-nailed dogs.

Hold your pup steady as you begin trimming his nails; you do not want him to make any sudden movements or run away. Talk to him soothingly and stroke him as you clip. Holding his foot in your hand, simply take off the end of each nail with one swift clip. You should purchase nail clippers that

NAIL FILING
You can purchase an electric tool to grind down a dog's nails rather than cut them. Some dogs don't seem to mind the electric grinder but will object strongly to nail clippers. Your dog's reactions to the procedure will help you make the right choice.

are made for use on dogs; you can probably find them wherever you buy pet supplies.

TOOTH CARE
Teeth should always be kept clean and as free from tartar as possible. Tooth-brushing products are now made for dogs, including the basics, like toothbrushes and canine toothpaste. Make your home dental-care regimen part of your regular grooming routine.

Make brushing your Black Russian's teeth part of your regular grooming sessions.

TRAVELING WITH YOUR DOG

CAR TRAVEL

You should accustom your Black Russian Terrier to riding in a car at an early age. You may or may not take him in the car often, but at the very least he will need to go to the vet and you do not want these trips to be traumatic for the dog or troublesome for you. The safest way for a dog to ride in the car is in his crate. If he uses a crate in the house, you can use the same crate for travel, provided that your vehicle is large enough to accommodate his crate.

Put the pup in the crate and see how he reacts. If he seems uneasy, you can have a passenger hold him on his lap while you drive. Another option for car travel is a specially made safety harness for dogs, which straps the dog in much like a seat belt. Those with larger vehicles, like station wagons or sport utility vehicles, can partition the rear section of the vehicle to create an area of safe confinement for the dog. Whatever option you choose, never let the dog roam loose in the vehicle—this is very dangerous! If you should stop short, your dog can be thrown and injured. If the dog starts climbing on you and pestering you while you are driving, you will not be able to concentrate on the road. It is an unsafe situation for everyone—human and canine.

For long trips, be prepared to stop to let the dog relieve himself. Take with you whatever you need to clean up after him, including some paper towels and perhaps some old bath towels for use should he have a potty accident in the car or suffer from motion sickness.

AIR TRAVEL

Contact your chosen airline before proceeding with your travel plans that include your Black Russian

Select a conveniently located kennel with large, secure areas for the dogs and an attentive, caring staff. Perhaps your vet or other dog owners can give you recommendations.

Terrier. The dog will be required to travel in a fiberglass crate and you should always check in advance with the airline regarding specific requirements for the crate's size, type and labeling, as well as any travel restrictions, such as during summer months.

As you prepare to travel, you'll want to make your Blackie as comfortable as possible. To help put the dog at ease, give him one of his favorite toys in the crate. Do not feed the dog for several hours prior to checking in so that you minimize his need to relieve himself. However, some airlines require you to provide documentation as to when the dog has last been fed. In any case, a light meal is best. For long trips, you will have to attach food and water

bowls to the dog's crate so that airline employees can tend to him between legs of the trip.

Make sure that your dog is properly identified and that your contact information appears on his ID tags and on his crate. Your Black Russian Terrier will travel in a different area of the plane than the human passengers, so every rule must be followed to prevent the slight risk of getting separated from your dog.

VACATIONS AND BOARDING
So you want to take a family vacation—and you want to include *all* members of the family. You would probably make arrangements for accommodations ahead of time anyway, but this is especially important when travel-

ing with a dog, especially a large dog. You do not want to make an overnight stop at the only place around for miles, only to find out that they do not allow dogs. Also, you do not want to reserve a place for your family without confirming that you are traveling with a dog because, if it is against the hotel's policy, you may end up without a place to stay.

Alternatively, if you are traveling and choose not to bring your Black Russian Terrier, you will have to make arrangements for him while you are away. Some options are to take him to stay with a friend that he knows well while you are gone, to have a familiar and trusted friend stay at your house or to bring your dog to a reputable boarding kennel. If you choose to board him at a kennel, you should visit in advance to see the facilities provided and where the dogs are kept. Are the dogs' areas spacious and kept clean? Talk to some of the employees and observe how they treat the dogs—do they spend

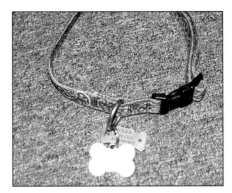

Your Black Russian Terrier should never be without his identification tags securely fastened to his everyday collar.

time with the dogs, play with them, exercise them, etc.? Also find out the kennel's policy on vaccinations and what they require. This is for all of the dogs' safety, since there is a greater risk of diseases being passed from dog to dog when dogs are kept together.

IDENTIFICATION

Your Black Russian Terrier is your valued companion and friend. That is why you always keep a close eye on him and you have made sure that he cannot escape from the yard or wriggle out of his collar and run away from you. However, accidents can happen and there may come a time when your dog unexpectedly becomes separated from you. If this unfortunate event should occur, the first thing on your mind will be finding him. Proper identification, including an ID tag and possibly a tattoo and/or microchip, will increase the chances of his being returned to you safely.

TRAVEL TIP

Never leave your dog alone in the car. In hot weather, your dog can die from the high temperature inside a closed vehicle; even a car parked in the shade can heat up very quickly. Leaving the window open is dangerous as well since the dog can hurt himself trying to get out.

TRAINING YOUR

BLACK RUSSIAN TERRIER

Living with an untrained dog is a lot like owning a piano that you do not know how to play—it is a nice object to look at, but it does not do much more than that to bring you pleasure. Now try taking piano lessons, and suddenly the piano comes alive and brings forth magical sounds and rhythms that set your heart singing and your body swaying.

The same is true with your Black Russian Terrier. Any dog is a big responsibility and, if not trained sensibly, may develop unacceptable behavior that annoys you or could even cause family friction.

To train your Black Russian Terrier, you may like to enroll in an obedience class. Teach your dog good manners as you learn how and why he behaves the way he does. Find out how to communicate with your dog and how to recognize and understand his communications with you. Suddenly the dog takes on a new role in your life—he is clever, interesting, well behaved and fun to be with. He demonstrates his bond of devotion to you daily. In other words, your Black Russian Terrier does

wonders for your ego because he constantly reminds you that you are not only his leader, you are his hero!

Those involved with teaching dog obedience and counseling owners about their dogs' behavior have discovered some interesting facts about dog ownership. For example, training dogs when they are puppies results in the highest rate of success in developing well-mannered and well-adjusted adult dogs. Training an older dog, from six months to six years of age, can produce almost equal results, providing that the owner accepts the dog's slower rate of learning capability and is willing to work patiently to help the dog succeed at developing to his fullest potential. Unfortunately, many owners of untrained adult dogs lack the patience factor, so

SPECIALIZED WORK
Bred as a working dog, the BRT in some countries is trained in defense work and has earned the reputation of being a "man-stopper." The breed can also be used as rescue dogs and as sniffer dogs.

they do not persist until their dogs are successful at learning particular behaviors.

Training a puppy aged 10 to 16 weeks (20 weeks at the most) is like working with a dry sponge in a pool of water. The pup soaks up whatever you show him and constantly looks for more things to do and learn. At this early age, his body is not yet producing hormones, and therein lies the reason for such a high rate of success. Without hormones, he is focused on his owners and not particularly interested in investigating other places, dogs, people, etc. You are his leader: his provider of food, water, shelter and security. He latches onto you and wants to stay close. He will usually follow you from room to room, will not let you out of his sight when you are outdoors with him and will respond in like manner to the people and animals you encounter. If you greet a friend warmly, he will be happy to

greet the person as well. If, however, you are hesitant or anxious about the approach of a stranger, he will respond accordingly.

Once the puppy begins to produce hormones, his natural curiosity emerges and he begins to investigate the world around him. It is at this time when you may notice that the untrained dog begins to wander away from you and even ignore your

The Black Russian Terrier is an intelligent and capable dog; a dog with a world of potential just waiting to be developed to his fullest through your training and guidance.

CANINE DEVELOPMENT SCHEDULE

It is important to understand how and at what age a puppy develops into adulthood. If you are a puppy owner, consult the following Canine Development Schedule to determine the stage of development your puppy is currently experiencing. This knowledge will help you as you work with the puppy in the weeks and months ahead.

Period	Age	Characteristics
First to Third	**Birth to Seven Weeks**	Puppy needs food, sleep and warmth, and responds to simple and gentle touching. Needs mother for security and disciplining. Needs littermates for learning and interacting with other dogs. Pup learns to function within a pack and learns pack order of dominance. Begin socializing pup with adults and children for short periods. Pup begins to become aware of his environment.
Fourth	**Eight to Twelve Weeks**	Brain is fully developed. Needs socializing with outside world. Remove from mother and littermates. Needs to change from canine pack to human pack. Human dominance necessary. Fear period occurs between 8 and 12 weeks. Avoid fright and pain.
Fifth	**Thirteen to Sixteen Weeks**	Training and formal obedience should begin. Less association with other dogs, more with people, places, situations. Period will pass easily if you remember this is pup's change-to-adolescence time. Be firm and fair. Flight instinct prominent. Permissiveness and over-disciplining can do permanent damage. Praise for good behavior.
Juvenile	**Four to Eight Months**	Another fear period about 7 to 8 months of age. It passes quickly, but be cautious of fright and pain. Sexual maturity reached. Dominant traits established. Dog should understand sit, down, come and stay by now.

Note: These are approximate time frames. Allow for individual differences in puppies.

commands to stay close. When this behavior becomes a problem, you have two choices: get rid of the dog or train him. It is strongly urged that you choose the latter option.

You usually will be able to find obedience classes within a reasonable distance from your home, but you can also do a lot to train your dog yourself. Sometimes there are classes available, but the tuition is too costly. Whatever the circumstances, the solution to training your dog without formal obedience classes lies within the pages of this book.

This chapter is devoted to helping you train your Black Russian Terrier at home. If the recommended procedures are followed faithfully, you may expect positive results that will prove rewarding to both you and your dog.

Whether your new charge is a puppy or a mature adult, the methods of teaching and the techniques we use in training basic behaviors are the same. After all, no dog, whether puppy or adult, likes harsh or inhumane methods. All creatures, however, respond favorably to gentle motivational methods and sincere praise and encouragement. Now let us get started.

HOUSEBREAKING

You can train a puppy to relieve himself wherever you choose, but this must be somewhere suitable. You should bear in mind from the outset that when your puppy is old enough to go out in public places, any canine droppings must be removed at once. You will always have to carry with you a

REAP THE REWARDS
If you start with a normal, healthy dog and give him time, patience and some carefully executed lessons, you will reap the rewards of that training for the life of the dog. And what a life it will be! The two of you will find immeasurable pleasure in the companionship you have built together with love, respect and understanding.

small plastic bag or "poop-scoop."

Outdoor training includes such surfaces as grass, soil and cement. Indoor training usually means training your dog to newspaper, not a viable option with a large breed like the Blackie. When deciding on the surface and location that you will want your Black Russian Terrier to use, be sure it is going to be permanent. Training your dog to grass and then changing your mind a few months later is extremely difficult for both dog and owner.

Next, choose the command you will use each and every time you want your puppy to void. "Hurry up" and "Let's go" are examples of commands commonly used by dog owners. Get in the habit of giving the puppy your chosen relief command before you take him out. That way, when he becomes an adult, you will be able to determine if he wants to

Potty accidents are a fact of life when you're a puppy owner. Don't become angry with the pup, and remember that the time of accidents will soon pass, if you are diligent in your housebreaking efforts.

> ## THE CLEAN LIFE
> By providing sleeping and resting quarters that fit the dog, and offering frequent opportunities to relieve himself outside his quarters, the puppy quickly learns that the outdoors is the place to go when he needs to urinate or defecate. It also reinforces his innate desire to keep his sleeping quarters clean. This, in turn, helps develop the muscle control that will eventually produce a dog with clean living habits.

go out when you ask him. A confirmation will be signs of interest, such as wagging his tail, watching you intently, going to the door, etc.

PUPPY'S NEEDS
The puppy needs to relieve himself after play periods, after each meal, after he has been sleeping and at any time he indicates that he is looking for a place to urinate or defecate. The urinary and intestinal tract muscles of very young puppies are not fully developed. Therefore, like human babies, puppies need to relieve themselves frequently.

Take your puppy out often— every hour for an eight-week-old, for example—and always immediately after sleeping and eating. The older the puppy, the less often he will need to relieve himself. Finally, as a mature

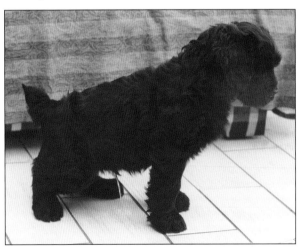

healthy adult, he will require only three to five relief trips per day.

HOUSING

Since the types of housing and control you provide for your puppy have a direct relationship on the success of housebreaking, we consider the various aspects of both before we begin training.

Taking a new puppy home and turning him loose in your house can be compared to turning a child loose in an amusement park and telling the child that the place is all his! The sheer enormity of the place would be too much for him to handle. Instead, offer the puppy clearly defined areas where he can play, sleep, eat and live. A room of the house where the family gathers is the most obvious choice. Puppies are social animals and need to feel a part of the pack right from the start. Hearing your voice, watching you while you are doing things and smelling you nearby are all positive reinforcers that he is now a member of your pack. Usually a family room, the kitchen or a nearby adjoining breakfast area is ideal for providing safety and security for both puppy and owner.

Within the designated room, there should be a smaller area that the puppy can call his own. An alcove, a wire or fiberglass dog crate or a partitioned (not boarded!) corner from which he

HOW MANY TIMES A DAY?

AGE	RELIEF TRIPS
To 14 weeks	10
14–22 weeks	8
22–32 weeks	6
Adulthood	4
(dog stops growing)	

These are estimates, of course, but they are a guide to the *minimum* number of opportunities a dog should have each day to relieve himself.

can view the activities of his new family will be fine. The size of the area or crate is the key factor here. The area must be large enough so that the puppy can lie down and stretch out, as well as stand up, without rubbing his head on the top. At the same time, it must be small enough so that he cannot relieve himself at one end and sleep at the other without coming into contact with his droppings before he is fully trained to relieve himself outside. Dogs are, by nature, clean animals and will not remain close to their relief areas unless forced to do so. In those cases, they then become dirty dogs and usually remain that way for life.

The dog's designated area should contain clean bedding and a toy. It is not advised to put food or water in the dog's crate during the housebreaking process, as eating and drinking will activate his digestive processes and ulti-mately defeat your purpose, as well as make the puppy very uncomfortable as he attempts to "hold it."

CONTROL

By *control*, we mean helping the puppy to create a lifestyle pattern that will be compatible to that of his human pack (*you!*). Just as we guide little children to learn our way of life, we must show the puppy when it is time to play, eat, sleep, exercise and even entertain himself.

Your puppy should always sleep in his crate. He should also learn that, during times of house-hold confusion and excessive human activity, such as at break-fast when family members are preparing for the day, he can play by himself in relative safety and comfort in his designated area. Each time you leave the puppy alone, he should understand exactly where he is to stay.

Puppies are chewers. They cannot tell the difference between what is safe to chew on and inap-propriate items like lamp and television wires, shoes, table legs, etc. Chewing into a television wire, for example, can be fatal to the puppy, while a shorted wire can start a fire in the house. If the puppy chews on the arm of the chair when he is alone, you will probably discipline him angrily when you get home. Thus, he makes the association that your

MEALTIME

Mealtime should be a peaceful time for your puppy. Do not put his food and water bowls in a high-traffic area in the house. For example, give him his own little corner of the kitchen where he can eat undisturbed and where he will not be underfoot. Do not allow small children or other family members to disturb the pup when he is eating.

coming home means he is going to be punished. (He will not remember chewing the chair and is incapable of making the association of the discipline with his naughty deed.) Accustoming the pup to his designated area not only keeps him safe but also avoids his engaging in destructive behaviors when you are not around.

Times of excitement, such as special occasions, family parties, etc., can be fun for the puppy, providing that he can view the activities from the security of his designated area. He is not underfoot and he is not being fed all sorts of tidbits that will probably cause him stomach distress, yet he still feels a part of the fun.

SCHEDULE

A puppy should be taken to his relief area each time he is released from his designated area, after meals, after play sessions and when he first awakens in the morning (at age eight weeks, this can mean 5 a.m.!). The puppy will indicate that he's ready "to go" by

circling or sniffing busily—do not misinterpret these signs. For a puppy less than ten weeks of age, a routine of taking him out every hour is necessary. As the puppy grows, he will be able to wait for longer periods of time.

Keep trips to his relief area short. Stay no more than five or six minutes and then return to the house. If he goes during that time, praise him lavishly and take him indoors immediately. If he does not, but he has an accident when you go back indoors, pick him up immediately, say "No! No!" and

Your young BRT is an eager student, waiting to absorb every lesson you teach him.

Always clean up after your dog, whether you are in a public place or your own yard.

return to his relief area. Wait a few minutes, then return to the house again. Never hit a puppy or put his face in urine or excrement when he has had an accident!

Once indoors, put the puppy in his crate until you have had time to clean up his accident. Then, release him to the family area and watch him more closely than before. Chances are, his accident was a result of your not picking up his signal or waiting too long before offering him the opportunity to relieve himself. Never hold a grudge against the puppy for accidents.

Let the puppy learn that going outdoors means it is time to relieve himself, not to play. Once

THE SUCCESS METHOD

Success that comes by luck is usually short-lived. Success that comes by well-thought-out proven methods is often more easily achieved and permanent. This is the Success Method. It is designed to give you, the puppy owner, a simple yet proven way to help your puppy develop clean living habits and a feeling of security in his new environment.

6 Steps to Successful Crate Training

1 Tell the puppy "Crate time!" and place him in the crate with a small treat (a piece of cheese or half of a biscuit). Let him stay in the crate for five minutes while you are in the same room. Then release him and praise lavishly. Never release him when he is fussing. Wait until he is quiet before you let him out.

2 Repeat Step 1 several times a day.

3 The next day, place the puppy in the crate as before. Let him stay there for ten minutes. Do this several times.

4 Continue building time in five-minute increments until the puppy stays in his crate for 30 minutes with you in the room. Always take him to his relief area after prolonged periods in his crate.

5 Now go back to Step 1 and let the puppy stay in his crate for five minutes, this time while you are out of the room.

6 Once again, build crate time in five-minute increments with you out of the room. When the puppy will stay willingly in his crate (he may even fall asleep!) for 30 minutes with you out of the room, he will be ready to stay in it for several hours at a time.

trained, he will be able to play indoors and out and still differentiate between the times for play versus the times for relief. Help him develop regular hours for naps, being alone, playing by himself and just resting, all in his crate. Encourage him to entertain himself while you are busy with your activities. Let him learn that having you near is comforting, but it is not your main purpose in life to provide him with your undivided attention.

Each time you put your puppy in his own area, use the same command, whatever suits best. Soon he will run to his crate or special area when he hears you say those words. Crate training provides safety for you, the puppy and the home. It also provides the puppy with a feeling of security, and that helps the puppy achieve self-confidence and clean habits.

Remember that one of the primary ingredients in housebreaking your puppy is control. Regardless of your lifestyle, there will always be occasions when you will need to have a place where your dog can stay and be happy and safe. Crate training is the answer for now and in the future.

In conclusion, a few key elements are really all you need for a successful housebreaking method—consistency, frequency, praise, control and supervision. By following these procedures

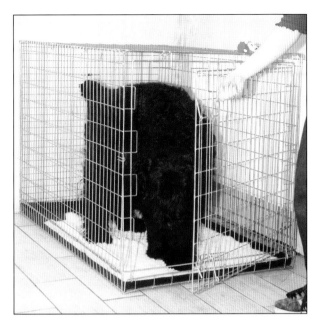

with a normal, healthy puppy, you and the puppy will soon be past the stage of accidents and ready to move on to a clean and rewarding life together.

ROLES OF DISCIPLINE, REWARD AND PUNISHMENT

Discipline, training one to act in accordance with rules, brings order to life. It is as simple as that. Without discipline, particularly in a group society, chaos will reign supreme and the group will eventually perish. Humans and canines are social animals and need some form of discipline in order to function effectively. They must procure food, reproduce to keep their species going and protect their home base and their

Start crate training with your Black Russian as a pup, and you will have an adult dog who willingly accepts his crate and enjoys having his own special place in the home.

> ## THINK BEFORE YOU BARK
> Dogs are sensitive to their masters' moods and emotions. Use your voice wisely when communicating with your dog. Never raise your voice at your dog unless you are trying to correct him. "Barking" at your dog can become as meaningless as "dogspeak" is to you.

young. If there were no discipline in the lives of social animals, they would eventually die from starvation and/or predation by other stronger animals. In the case of domestic canines, discipline in their lives is needed in order for them to understand how their pack (you and other family members) functions and how they must act in order to survive.

A large humane society in a highly populated area recently surveyed dog owners regarding their satisfaction with their relationships with their dogs. People who had trained their dogs were 75% more satisfied with their pets than those who had never trained their dogs.

Renowned psychologist Dr. Edward Thorndike established *Thorndike's Theory of Learning*, which states that a behavior that results in a pleasant event tends to be repeated. Furthermore, it concludes that a behavior that results in an unpleasant event tends not to be repeated. It is this theory upon which training methods are based today. For example,

if you manipulate a dog to perform a specific behavior and reward him for doing it, he is likely to do it again because he enjoyed the end result.

Occasionally, punishment, a penalty inflicted for an offense, is necessary. The best type of punishment often comes from an outside source. For example, a child is told not to touch the stove because he may get burned. He disobeys and touches the stove. In doing so, he receives a burn. From that time on, he respects the heat of the stove and avoids contact with it. Therefore, a behavior that results in an unpleasant event tends not to be repeated.

A good example of a dog's learning the hard way is the dog who chases the house cat. He is told many times to leave the cat alone, yet he persists in teasing the cat. Then, one day, the dog begins chasing the cat but the cat turns and swipes a claw across the dog's face, leaving the dog with a painful gash on his nose. The final result is that the dog stops chasing the cat.

TRAINING EQUIPMENT

COLLAR AND LEASH
For a Black Russian Terrier, the collar and leash that you use for training must be one with which you are easily able to work, not too heavy for the dog and perfectly safe.

CALM DOWN

Dogs will do anything for your attention. If you reward the dog when he is calm and attentive, you will develop a well-mannered dog. If, on the other hand, you greet your dog excitedly and encourage him to wrestle with you, the dog will greet you the same way and you will have a hyperactive dog on your hands.

TREATS

Have a bag of treats on hand; something nutritious and easy to swallow works best. Use a soft treat, a chunk of cheese or a piece of cooked chicken rather than a dry biscuit. By the time the dog has finished chewing a dry treat, he will forget why he is being rewarded in the first place!

Incidentally, using food rewards will not teach a dog to beg at the table—the only way to teach a dog to beg at the table is to give him food from the table. In training, rewarding the dog with a food treat will help him associate praise and the treats with learning new behaviors that obviously please his owner.

TRAINING BEGINS: ASK THE DOG A QUESTION

In order to teach your dog anything, you must first get his attention. After all, he cannot learn anything if he is looking away from you with his mind on something else.

To get your dog's attention, ask him "School?" and immediately walk over to him and give him a treat as you tell him "Good dog." Wait a minute or two and repeat the routine, this time with a treat in your hand as you approach within a foot of the dog. Do not go directly to him, but stop about a foot short of him and hold out the treat as you ask "School?" He will see you approaching with a treat in your hand and most

Consistency in your daily routine is tantamount to teaching your dog proper behavior. This BRT has finished his business in the yard and waits politely by the door.

likely begin walking toward you. As you meet, give him the treat and praise again.

The third time, ask the question, have a treat in your hand and walk only a short distance toward the dog so that he must walk almost all the way to you. As he reaches you, give him the treat and praise again.

By this time, the dog will probably be getting the idea that if he pays attention to you, especially when you ask that question, it will pay off in treats and enjoyable activities for him. In other words, he learns that "school" means doing great things with you that are fun and that result in positive attention for him.

Remember that the dog does not understand your verbal language; he only recognizes sounds. Your question translates to a series of sounds for him, and those sounds become the signal to go to you and pay attention. The dog learns that if he does this, he will get to interact with you plus receive treats and praise.

THE BASIC COMMANDS

TEACHING SIT

Now that you have the dog's attention, attach his leash and hold it in your left hand, and hold a food treat in your right hand. Place your food hand at the dog's nose and let him lick the treat but not take it from you. Say "Sit" and slowly raise your food hand from in front of the dog's nose up over his head so that he is looking at the ceiling. As he bends his head upward, he will have to bend his knees to maintain his balance. As he bends his knees, he will assume a sit position. At that point, release the food treat and praise lavishly with comments such as "Good dog! Good sit!," etc. Remember to always praise enthusiastically, because dogs relish verbal praise from their owners and feel so proud of themselves whenever they accomplish a behavior.

You will not use food forever in getting the dog to obey your commands. Food is only used to teach new behaviors and, once the dog knows what you want when you give a specific command, you will wean him off the food treats but still maintain the verbal praise. After all, you will always have your voice with you, and there will be many times when you have no food rewards but expect the dog to obey.

HONOR AND OBEY
Dogs are the most honorable animals in existence. They consider another species (humans) as their own. They interface with you. You are their leader. Puppies perceive children to be on their level; their actions around small children are different from their behavior around their adult masters.

LANGUAGE BARRIER

Dogs do not understand our language and have to rely on tone of voice more than just words or sound. They can be trained to react to a certain sound, at a certain volume. If you say "No, Oliver" in a very soft, pleasant voice, it will not have the same meaning as "No, Oliver!!" when you raise your voice. You should never use the dog's name during a reprimand, just the command "No! " You never want the dog to associate his name with a negative experience or reprimand.

TEACHING DOWN

Teaching the down exercise is easy when you understand how the dog perceives the down position, and it is very difficult when you do not. Dogs perceive the down position as a submissive one; therefore, teaching the down exercise by using a forceful method can sometimes make the dog develop such a fear of the down that he either runs away when you say "Down" or he attempts to snap at the person who tries to force him down.

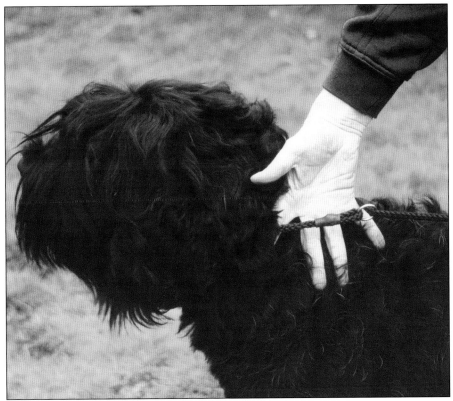

Proper training requires a proper collar and leash. Both should be lightweight yet strong, and of the proper size for your BRT.

Have the dog sit close along-side your left leg, facing in the same direction as you are. Hold the leash in your left hand and a food treat in your right. Now place your left hand lightly on the top of the dog's shoulders where they meet above the spinal cord. Do not push down on the dog's shoulders; simply rest your left hand there so you can guide the dog to lie down close to your left leg rather than to swing away from your side when he drops.

DOUBLE JEOPARDY

A dog in jeopardy never lies down. He stays alert on his feet because instinct tells him that he may have to run away or fight for his survival. Therefore, if a dog feels threatened or anxious, he will not lie down. Consequently, it is important to keep the dog calm and relaxed as he learns the down exercise.

Now place the food hand at the dog's nose, say "Down" very softly (almost a whisper) and slowly lower the food hand to the dog's front feet. When the food hand reaches the floor, begin moving it forward along the floor in front of the dog. Keep talking softly to the dog, saying things like, "Do you want this treat? You can do this, good dog." Your reas-suring tone of voice will help calm the dog as he tries to follow the food hand in order to get the treat.

When the dog's elbows touch the floor, release the food and praise softly. Try to get the dog to maintain that down position for several seconds before you let him sit up again. The goal here is to get the dog to settle down and not feel threatened in the down position.

TEACHING STAY

It is easy to teach the dog to stay in either a sit or a down position. Again, we use food and praise during the teaching process as we help the dog to understand exactly what it is that we are expecting him to do.

To teach the sit/stay, start with the dog sitting on your left side as before and hold the leash in your left hand. Have a food treat in your right hand and place your food hand at the dog's nose. Say "Stay" and step out on your right foot to stand directly in front

Teaching the sit is likely the first lesson you will teach your Black Russian. Sometimes a dog has to be guided gently into position for the first few times to understand what is expected of him.

of the dog, toe to toe, as he licks and nibbles the treat. Be sure to keep his head facing upward to maintain the sit position. Count to five and then swing around to stand next to the dog again with him on your left. As soon as you get back to the original position, release the food and praise lavishly.

To teach the down/stay, do the down as previously described. As soon as the dog lies down, say "Stay" and step out on your right foot just as you did in the sit/stay. Count to five and then return to stand beside the dog with him on your left side. Release the treat and praise as always.

Within a week or ten days,

you can begin to add a bit of distance between you and your dog when you leave him. When you do, use your left hand open with the palm facing the dog as a stay signal, much the same as the hand signal a police officer uses to stop traffic at an intersection. Hold the food treat in your right hand as before, but this time the food will not be touching the dog's nose. He will watch the food hand and quickly learn that he is going to get that treat as soon as you return to his side.

When you can stand 3 feet away from your dog for 30 seconds, you can then begin building time and distance in both stays. Eventually, the dog

You will find many situations in which it is useful to have your dog stay on command, so the time you put into teaching the lesson is well worth it.

FEAR AGGRESSION

Pups who are subjected to physical abuse during training commonly end up with behavioral problems as adults. One common result of abuse is fear aggression, in which a dog will lash out, bare his teeth, snarl and finally bite someone by whom he feels threatened. For example, your daughter may be playing with the dog one afternoon. As they play hide-and-seek, she backs the dog into a corner and, as she attempts to tease him playfully, he bites her hand. Examine the cause of this behavior. Did your daughter ever hit the dog? Did someone who resembles your daughter hit or scream at the dog?

Fortunately, fear aggression is relatively easy to correct. Have your daughter engage in only positive activities with the dog, such as feeding, petting and walking. She should not give any corrections or negative feedback. If the dog still growls or cowers away from her, allow someone else to accompany them. After approximately one week, the dog should feel that he can rely on her for many positive things, and he will also be prevented from reacting fearfully towards anyone who might resemble her.

---

can be expected to remain in the stay position for prolonged periods of time until you return to him or call him to you. Always praise lavishly when he stays.

TEACHING COME

If you make teaching "come" an exciting experience, you should never have a "student" that does not love the game or that fails to come when called. The secret, it seems, is never to teach the word "come."

At times when an owner most wants his dog to come when called, the owner is likely to be upset or anxious and he allows these feelings to come through in the tone of his voice when he calls his dog. Hearing that desperation in his owner's voice, the dog fears the results of going to him and therefore either disobeys outright or runs in the opposite direction. The secret, therefore, is to teach the dog a game and, when you want him to come to you, simply play the game. It is practically a no-fail solution!

To begin, have several members of your family take a few food treats and each go into a different room in the house. Everyone takes turns calling the dog, and each person should celebrate the dog's finding him with a treat and lots of happy praise. When a person calls the dog, he is actually inviting the dog to find him and to get a treat as a reward for "winning."

A few turns of the "Where are you?" game and the dog will understand that everyone is playing the game and that each person

"COME"...BACK

Never call your dog to come to you for a correction or scold him when he reaches you. That is the quickest way to turn a come command into "Go away fast!" Dogs think only in the present tense, and your dog will connect the scolding with coming to you, not with the misbehavior of a few moments earlier.

has a big celebration awaiting the dog's success at locating him or her. Once the dog learns to love the game, simply calling out "Where are you?" will bring him running from wherever he is when he hears that all-important question.

The come command is recognized as one of the most important things to teach a dog, but there are trainers who work with thousands of dogs and never use the actual word "come." Yet these dogs will race to respond to a person who uses the dog's name followed by "Where are you?" For example, a woman has a 12-year-old companion dog who went blind, but who never fails to locate her owner when asked, "Where are you?"

Children, in particular, love to play this game with their dogs. Children can hide in smaller places like a shower stall or bathtub, behind a bed or under a table. The dog needs to work a little bit harder to find these hiding places, but, when he does, he loves to celebrate with a treat and a tussle with a favorite youngster.

TEACHING HEEL

Heeling means that the dog walks beside the owner without pulling. It takes time and patience on the owner's part to succeed at teaching the dog that he (the owner) will not proceed unless the dog is walking calmly beside him.

COMMAND STANCE

Stand up straight and authoritatively when giving your dog commands. Do not issue commands when lying on the floor or lying on your back on the sofa. If you are on your hands and knees when you give a command, your dog will think you are positioning yourself to play.

will walk calmly beside you for three steps without pulling, increase the number of steps you take to five. When he will walk politely beside you while you take five steps, you can increase the length of your walk to ten steps. Keep increasing the length of your stroll until the dog will walk quietly beside you without pulling as long as you want him to heel. When you stop heeling, indicate to the dog that the exercise is over by verbally praising as you pet him and say "OK, good dog." The "OK" is used as a

Neither pulling out ahead on the leash nor lagging behind is acceptable.

Begin by holding the leash in your left hand as the dog sits beside your left leg. Move the loop end of the leash to your right hand, but keep your left hand short on the leash so that it keeps the dog in close next to you.

Say "Heel" and step forward on your left foot. Keep the dog close to you and take three steps. Stop and have the dog sit next to you in what we now call the heel position. Praise verbally, but do not touch the dog. Hesitate a moment and begin again with "Heel," taking three steps and stopping, at which point the dog is told to sit again.

Your goal here is to have the dog walk those three steps without pulling on the leash. Once he

A large dog like the Black Russian would surely take his owner for a walk, instead of the other way around, if not trained to heel.

Eventually, the dog will begin to respond and within a few days he will be walking politely beside you without pulling on the leash. At first, the training sessions should be kept short and very positive; soon the dog will be able to walk nicely with you for increasingly longer distances. Remember also to give the dog free time and the opportunity to run and play when you have finished heel practice.

WEANING OFF FOOD IN TRAINING

Food is used in training new behaviors. Once the dog understands what behavior goes with a specific command, it is time to

Two dogs mean twice the effort in training, but it's a double delight to have a pair of well-behaved Black Russian pals!

release word, meaning that the exercise is finished and the dog is free to relax.

If you are dealing with a dog who insists on pulling you around, simply "put on your brakes" and stand your ground until the dog realizes that the two of you are not going anywhere until he is beside you and moving at your pace, not his. It may take some time just standing there to convince the dog that you are the leader and that you will be the one to decide on the direction and speed of your travel.

Each time the dog looks up at you or slows down to give a slack leash between the two of you, quietly praise him and say "Good heel. Good dog."

SAFETY FIRST

While it may seem that the most important things to your dog are eating, sleeping and chewing the upholstery on your furniture, his first concern is actually safety. The domesticated dogs we keep as companions have the same pack instinct as their ancestors who ran free thousands of years ago. Because of this pack instinct, your dog wants to know that he and his pack are not in danger of being harmed, and that his pack has a strong, capable leader. You must establish yourself as the leader early on in your relationship. That way, your dog will trust that you will take care of him and the pack, and he will accept your commands without question.

start weaning him off the food treats. At first, give a treat after each exercise. Then, start to give a treat only after every *other* exercise. Mix up the times when you offer a food reward and the times when you offer only praise so that the dog will never know when he is going to receive both food and praise and when he is going to receive only praise. This is called a variable-ratio reward system. It proves successful because there is always the chance that the owner will produce a treat, so the dog never stops trying for that reward. No matter what, *always* give verbal praise.

OBEDIENCE CLASSES

It is a good idea to enroll in an obedience class if one is available in your area. If yours is a show dog, handling classes to prepare the two of you for the show ring would be more appropriate. Many areas have dog clubs that offer basic obedience training as well as preparatory classes for obedience competition. There are also local dog trainers who offer similar classes.

At obedience trials, dogs can earn titles at various levels of competition. The beginning levels of obedience competition include basic behaviors such as sit, down, heel, etc. The more advanced levels of competition

HOW TO WEAN THE "TREAT HOG"

If you have trained your dog by rewarding him with a treat each time he performs a command, he may soon decide that without the treat, he won't sit, stay or come. The best way to fix this problem is to start asking your dog to do certain commands twice before being rewarded. Slowly increase the number of commands given and then vary the number: three sits and a treat one day, five sits for a biscuit the next day, etc. Your dog will soon realize that there is no set number of sits before he gets his reward and he'll likely do it the first time you ask in the hope of being rewarded sooner rather than later.

include jumping, retrieving, scent discrimination and signal work. The advanced levels require a dog and owner to put a lot of time and effort into their training. The titles that can be earned at these levels of competition are very prestigious.

OTHER ACTIVITIES FOR LIFE

Whether a dog is trained in the structured environment of a class or alone with his owner at home, there are many activities that can bring fun and rewards to both owner and dog once they have mastered basic control.

Teaching the dog to help out around the home, in the yard or on the farm provides great satisfaction to both dog and owner. In addition, the dog's help makes life a little easier for his owner and raises his stature as a valued companion to his family. It helps give the dog a purpose by occupying his mind and providing an outlet for his energy.

Backpacking is an exciting and healthy activity that the dog can be taught without assistance from more than his owner. The exercise of walking and climbing is good for man and dog alike, and the bond that they develop together is priceless. The rule of thumb for backpacking with any dog is never to expect the dog to carry more than one-sixth of his body weight.

HELPING PAWS

Your dog may not be the next Lassie, but every pet has the potential to do some tricks well. Identify his natural talents and hone them. Is your dog always happy and upbeat? Teach him to wag his tail or give you his paw on command. Real homebodies can be trained to do household chores, such as carrying dirty laundry or retrieving the morning paper.

If you are interested in participating in organized competition with your Black Russian Terrier, there are activities other than obedience in which you and your dog can become involved. Agility is a popular sport in which dogs run through obstacle courses that include various jumps, tunnels and other exercises to test the dog's speed and coordination. The owners run beside their dogs to give commands and to guide them through the course. Although competitive, the focus is on fun—it's fun to do, fun to watch and great exercise.

As a Black Russian Terrier owner, you have the opportunity to participate in Schutzhund competition if you choose. Schutzhund originated as a test to determine the best-quality dogs to be used for breeding stock. Breeders continue to use it as a way to evaluate working ability and temperament. There are three levels in Schutzhund trials: SchH. I, SchH. II and SchH. III, with each level being progressively more difficult to complete successfully. Each level consists of training, obedience and protection phases. Training for Schutzhund is intense and must be practiced consistently to keep the dog keen. The experience of Schutzhund training is very rewarding for dog and owner, and the BRT's tractability is well suited for this type of training.

Conformation showing is one of the activities you can try with your Black Russian. Look at this dog's focus, as all of his attention is concentrated on his handler.

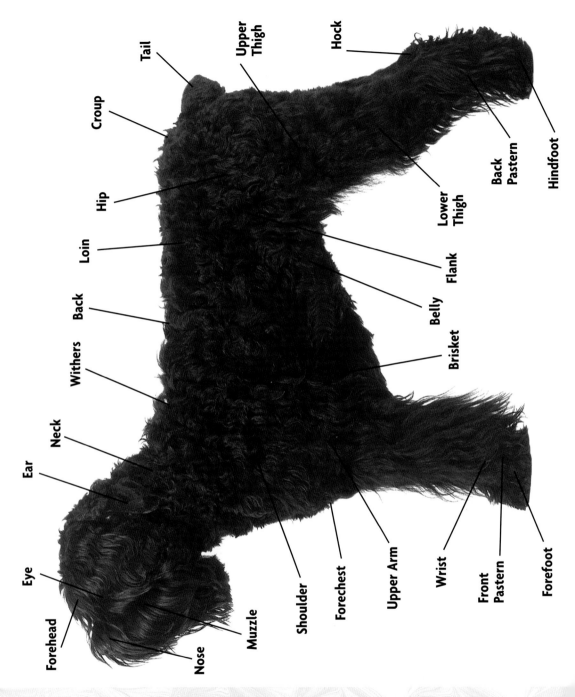

PHYSICAL STRUCTURE OF THE BLACK RUSSIAN TERRIER

BLACK RUSSIAN TERRIER

Dogs suffer from many of the same physical illnesses as people and might even share many of the same psychological problems. Since people usually know more about human diseases than canine maladies, many of the terms used in this chapter will be familiar but not necessarily those used by veterinarians. For example, we will use the familiar term *x-ray* instead of *radiograph*. We will also use the familiar term *symptoms*, even though dogs don't have symptoms, which are verbal descriptions of something the patient feels or observes himself that he regards as abnormal. Dogs have *clinical signs* since they cannot speak, so we have to look for these clinical signs…but we still use the term *symptoms* in the book.

Medicine is a constantly changing art, with of course scientific input as well. Things alter as we learn more and more about basic sciences such as genetics and biochemistry, and have use of more sophisticated imaging techniques like Computer Aided Tomography (CAT scans) or Magnetic Resonance Imaging (MRI scans). There is academic dispute about many canine maladies, so different veterinarians may treat them in different ways. For example, some vets place a greater emphasis on surgical treatments than others.

SELECTING A VETERINARIAN
Your selection of a veterinarian should be based on personal recommendation for his skills with dogs, and, if possible, especially large breeds. If the vet is based nearby, it will be helpful because you might have an emergency or need to make multiple visits for treatments.

All veterinarians should be licensed and capable of dealing with routine medical issues such as infections, injuries and the promotion of health (for example, by vaccination), and routine surgery such as neutering, stitching wounds and docking tails. If the problem affecting your dog is more complex, your vet will refer your pet to someone with a more detailed knowledge of what is wrong. This will usually be a specialist who concentrates in the relevant field (veterinary dermatology, veterinary ophthalmology, etc.).

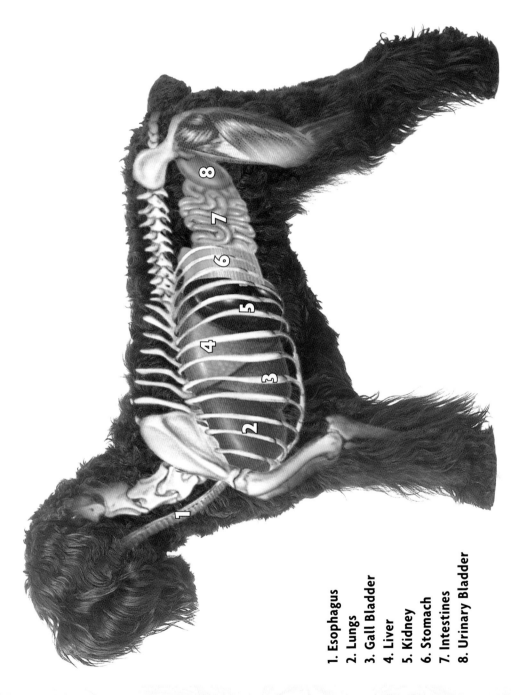

1. Esophagus
2. Lungs
3. Gall Bladder
4. Liver
5. Kidney
6. Stomach
7. Intestines
8. Urinary Bladder

INTERNAL ORGANS OF THE BLACK RUSSIAN TERRIER

Veterinary procedures are very costly and, as the treatments available improve, they are going to become more expensive. It is quite acceptable to discuss matters of cost with your vet; if there is more than one treatment option, cost may be a factor in deciding which route to take.

Insurance against veterinary cost is also becoming very popular. Some types of insurance cover the costs of unexpected emergencies such as surgery after a car accident, while more extensive policies can cover routine health care such as check-ups and flea control.

PREVENTATIVE MEDICINE

It is much easier, less costly and more effective to practice preventative medicine than to fight bouts of illness and disease. Properly bred puppies of all breeds come from parents that were selected based upon their genetic-disease profiles. The puppies' mother should have been vaccinated, free of all internal and external parasites and properly nourished. For these reasons, a visit to the veterinarian who cared for the dam is recommended if at all possible. The dam passes disease resistance to her puppies, which should last from eight to ten weeks. Unfortunately, she can also pass on parasites and infection. This is why knowledge about her health is useful in learning more about the health of the puppies.

WEANING TO FIVE MONTHS OLD

Puppies should be weaned by the time they are two months old. A puppy that remains for at least eight weeks with his mother and littermates usually adapts better to other dogs and people later in life.

Sometimes new owners have their puppy examined by a veterinarian immediately, before even bringing the pup home, which is a good idea unless the puppy is overtired by a long journey. In that case, the appointment should be made for the following day.

The puppy will have his teeth examined and have his skeletal conformation and general health checked prior to certification by the veterinarian. Puppies in certain breeds may have problems with their kneecaps, cataracts and other eye problems, heart murmurs and undescended testicles. Your vet might also have training in temperament testing and evaluation. At the first veterinary visit, the vet will set up a schedule for your pup's vaccinations.

VACCINATIONS

Most vaccinations are given by injection and should only be given by a veterinarian. Both he and you should keep a record of the date of the injection, the identification of the vaccine and the amount given. Some vets give a first vaccination at eight weeks, but most dog breeders prefer the course not to

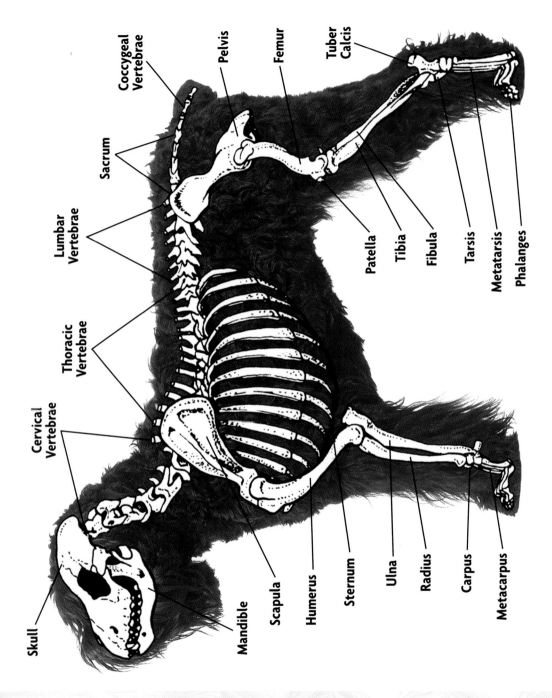

Coccygeal Vertebrae

Pelvis

Femur

Tuber Calcis

Sacrum

Lumbar Vertebrae

Thoracic Vertebrae

Cervical Vertebrae

Patella

Tibia

Fibula

Tarsis

Metatarsis

Phalanges

Skull

Mandible

Scapula

Humerus

Sternum

Ulna

Radius

Carpus

Metacarpus

SKELETAL STRUCTURE OF THE BLACK RUSSIAN TERRIER

commence until about ten weeks because of the risk of interaction with the antibodies produced by the mother. The vaccination schedule is usually based on a 15-day cycle. You must take your vet's advice as to when to vaccinate, as this may differ according to the vaccine used.

The usual vaccines contain immunizing doses of several different viruses such as distemper, parvovirus, parainfluenza and hepatitis. There are other vaccines available when the puppy is at risk. You should rely upon professional advice. This is especially true for the booster immunizations. Most vaccination programs require a booster when the puppy is a year old and once a year thereafter. In some cases, circumstances may require more or less frequent immunizations.

Canine cough, more formally known as tracheobronchitis, is immunized against with a vaccine that is sprayed into the dog's nostrils. Canine cough is usually included in routine vaccination, but it is often not as effective as the vaccines for other major diseases.

DISEASE REFERENCE CHART

	What is it?	What causes it?	Symptoms
Leptospirosis	Severe disease that affects the internal organs; can be spread to people.	A bacterium, which is often carried by rodents, that enters through mucous membranes and spreads quickly throughout the body.	Range from fever, vomiting and loss of appetite in less severe cases to shock, irreversible kidney damage and possibly death in most severe cases.
Rabies	Potentially deadly virus that infects warm-blooded mammals.	Bite from a carrier of the virus, mainly wild animals.	1st stage: dog exhibits change in behavior, fear. 2nd stage: dog's behavior becomes more aggressive. 3rd stage: loss of coordination, trouble with bodily functions.
Parvovirus	Highly contagious virus, potentially deadly.	Ingestion of the virus, which is usually spread through the feces of infected dogs.	Most common: severe diarrhea. Also vomiting, fatigue, lack of appetite.
Canine cough	Contagious respiratory infection.	Combination of types of bacteria and virus. Most common: *Bordetella bronchiseptica* bacteria and parainfluenza virus.	Chronic cough.
Distemper	Disease primarily affecting respiratory and nervous system.	Virus that is related to the human measles virus.	Mild symptoms such as fever, lack of appetite and mucus secretion progress to evidence of brain damage, "hard pad."
Hepatitis	Virus primarily affecting the liver.	Canine adenovirus type I (CAV-1). Enters system when dog breathes in particles.	Lesser symptoms include listlessness, diarrhea, vomiting. More severe symptoms include "blue-eye" (clumps of virus in eye).
Coronavirus	Virus resulting in digestive problems.	Virus is spread through infected dog's feces.	Stomach upset evidenced by lack of appetite, vomiting, diarrhea.

Normal hairs of a dog enlarged 200 times original size. The cuticle (outer covering) is clean and healthy. Unlike human hair that grows from the base, a dog's hair also grows from the end. Damaged hairs and split ends, illustrated above.

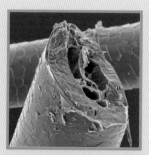
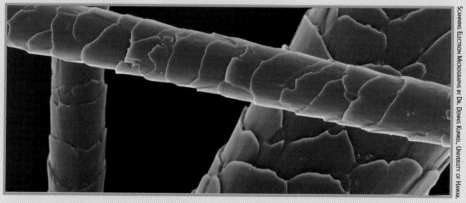

SCANNING ELECTRON MICROGRAPHS BY DR. DENNIS KUNKEL, UNIVERSITY OF HAWAII.

FIVE MONTHS TO ONE YEAR OF AGE

Unless you intend to breed or show your dog, neutering (males) or spaying (females) the puppy is recommended. Discuss this with your veterinarian. Opinions differ regarding the best age at which to have the procedure performed, but around six months is usual. Neutering and spaying have proven to be extremely beneficial to male and female dogs. Besides eliminating the possibility of pregnancy, it inhibits (but does not prevent) breast cancer in bitches and prostate cancer in male dogs.

Your veterinarian should provide your puppy with a thorough dental evaluation at six months of age, ascertaining whether all of the permanent teeth have erupted properly. A home dental-care regimen should be initiated at six months, including brushing weekly and providing good dental devices (such as hard plastic or nylon bones). Regular dental care promotes healthy teeth, fresh breath and a longer life.

DOGS OLDER THAN ONE YEAR

Continue to visit the veterinarian at least once a year. There is no such disease as "old age," but bodily functions do change with age. The eyes and ears are no longer as efficient. Liver, kidney and intestinal functions often decline. Proper dietary changes, recommended by your veterinarian, can make life more pleasant for your aging Black Russian Terrier and you.

SKIN PROBLEMS

Veterinarians are consulted by dog owners for skin problems more than for any other group of diseases or maladies. A dog's skin is as sensitive, if not more so, than human skin, and both suffer from almost the same ailments (though the occurrence of acne in most breeds is rare). For this reason, veterinary dermatology has developed into a specialty practiced by many veterinarians.

Since many skin problems have visual symptoms that are almost identical, it requires the skill of an experienced veterinary dermatologist to identify and cure many of the more severe skin disorders. Pet shops sell many treatments for skin problems, but most of the treatments are directed at symptoms and not at the underlying problem(s). If your dog is suffering from a skin disorder, you should seek professional assistance

HEALTH AND VACCINATION SCHEDULE

AGE IN WEEKS:	6TH	8TH	10TH	12TH	14TH	16TH	20-24TH	52ND
Worm Control	✔	✔	✔	✔	✔	✔	✔	
Neutering							✔	
Heartworm		✔		✔		✔	✔	
Parvovirus	✔		✔		✔		✔	✔
Distemper		✔		✔		✔		✔
Hepatitis		✔		✔		✔		✔
Leptospirosis								✔
Parainfluenza	✔		✔		✔			✔
Dental Examination		✔					✔	✔
Complete Physical		✔					✔	✔
Coronavirus				✔			✔	✔
Canine Cough	✔							
Hip Dysplasia								✔
Rabies							✔	

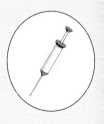

Vaccinations are not instantly effective. It takes about two weeks for the dog's immune system to develop antibodies. Most vaccinations require annual booster shots. Your vet should guide you in this regard.

as quickly as possible. As with all diseases, the earlier a problem is identified and treated, the more successful can be the cure.

HEREDITARY SKIN DISORDERS
Veterinary dermatologists are currently researching a number of skin disorders that are believed to have a hereditary basis. These inherited diseases are transmitted by both parents, who appear (phenotypically) normal but have a recessive gene for the disease, meaning that they carry, but are not affected by, the disease. These diseases pose serious problems to breeders because in some instances there are no methods of identifying carriers. Often the secondary diseases associated with these skin conditions are even more debilitating than the skin disorders themselves, including cancers and respiratory problems.

Among the hereditary skin disorders, for which the mode of inheritance is known, are acrodermatitis, cutaneous asthenia (Ehlers-Danlos syndrome), sebaceous adenitis, cyclic hematopoiesis, dermatomyositis, IgA deficiency, color dilution alopecia and nodular dermatofibrosis. Some of these disorders are limited to one or two breeds, while others affect a large number of breeds. All inherited diseases must be diagnosed and treated by a qualified veterinary specialist.

PARASITE BITES
Many of us are allergic to insect bites. The bites itch, erupt and may even become infected. Dogs have the same reaction to fleas, ticks and/or mites. When an insect lands on you, you have the chance to whisk it away with your hand. Unfortunately, when a dog is bitten by a flea, tick or mite, he can only scratch it away or bite it. By the time the dog has been bitten, the parasite has done some of its damage. It may also have laid eggs, which will cause further problems in the near future. The itching from parasite bites is probably due to the saliva injected into the site when the parasite sucks the dog's blood.

AIRBORNE ALLERGIES
Just as humans suffer from hay fever during the pollinating season, many dogs suffer from the same allergies. When the pollen count is high, your dog might suffer, but don't expect him to sneeze and have a runny nose as a human would. Dogs react to pollen allergies in the same way they react to fleas—they scratch and bite themselves. Dogs, like humans, can be tested for allergens. Discuss the testing with your veterinarian.

ACRAL LICK GRANULOMA
Many large dogs have a very poorly understood syndrome called acral lick granuloma. The manifestation of the problem is the dog's tireless attack at a specific area of the body,

almost always the legs or paws. The dog licks so intensively that he removes the hair and skin, leaving an ugly, large wound. Tiny protuberances, which are outgrowths of new capillaries, bead on the surface of the wound. Owners who notice their dogs' biting and chewing at their extremities should have the vet determine the cause. If lick granuloma is identified, although there is no absolute cure, corticosteroids are the most common treatment.

AUTO-IMMUNE ILLNESSES
An auto-immune illness is one in which the immune system overacts and does not recognize parts of the affected person; rather, the immune system starts to react as if these parts were foreign and need to be destroyed. An example is rheumatoid arthritis, which occurs when the body does not recognize the joints, thus leading to a very painful and damaging reaction in the joints. This has nothing to do with age, so can occur in children and young dogs. The wear-and-tear arthritis of the older person or dog is osteoarthritis.

Lupus is an auto-immune disease that affects dogs as well as people. It can take variable forms, affecting the kidneys, bones and the skin. It can be fatal, so is treated with steroids, which can themselves have very significant side effects. The steroids calm down the allergic reaction to the body's tissues, which helps the lupus, but they also decrease the body's reaction to real foreign substances such as bacteria, and also thin the skin and bones.

FOOD PROBLEMS

FOOD ALLERGIES
Some dogs can be allergic to many foods that may be best-sellers and highly recommended by breeders and vets. Changing the brand of food that you buy may not eliminate the problem if the element to which the dog is allergic is contained in the new brand.

Recognizing a food allergy in a dog can be difficult. Humans often have rashes when we eat foods to which we are allergic, or have swelling of the lips or eyes. Dogs do not usually develop rashes, but react in the same way as they do to an airborne or bite allergy—they itch, scratch and bite. While pollen allergies are usually seasonal, food allergies are year-round problems.

TREATING FOOD ALLERGIES
Diagnosis of food allergy is based on a two- to four-week dietary trial with a home-cooked diet fed to the exclusion of all other foods. The diet should consist of boiled rice or potato with a source of protein that the dog has never eaten before, such as fresh or frozen fish, lamb or even something as exotic as pheasant. Water has to be the only drink, and it is really important that no

other foods are fed during this trial. If the dog's condition improves, you will need to try the original diet once again to see if the itching resumes. If it does, then this confirms the diagnosis that the dog is allergic to his original diet. The treatment is long-term feeding of something that does not distress the dog's skin, which may be in the form of one of the commercially available hypoallergenic diets or the home-made diet that you created for the allergy trial.

FOOD INTOLERANCE

Food intolerance is the inability of the dog to completely digest certain foods. This occurs because the dog does not have the chemi-cals necessary to digest some food-stuffs. These chemicals are called enzymes. All puppies have the enzymes necessary to digest canine milk, but some dogs do not have the enzymes to digest a very different form of milk that is commonly found in human house-holds—milk from cows. In such dogs, drinking cows' milk results in loose bowels, stomach pains and the passage of gas.

Dogs often do not have the enzymes to digest soy or other beans. The treatment is to exclude the foodstuffs that upset your Black Russian Terrier's digestion.

BLOAT OR GASTRIC TORSION

This is a serious problem found in the large, deep-chested breeds.

DETECTING BLOAT

The following are symptoms of bloat and require *immediate* veterinary attention:

- Your dog's stomach starts to distend, ending up large and as tight as a football;
- Your dog is dribbling, as no saliva can be swallowed;
- Your dog makes frequent attempts to vomit but cannot bring anything up due to the stomach's being closed off;
- Your dog is distressed from pain;
- Your dog starts to suffer from clinical shock, meaning that there is not enough blood in the dog's circulation as the hard, dilated stomach stops the blood from returning to the heart to be pumped around the body. Clinical shock is indicated by pale gums and tongue, as they have been starved of blood. The shocked dog also has glazed, staring eyes.

You have minutes—yes, *minutes*—to get your dog into surgery. If you see any of these symptoms at any time of the day or night, get to the vet's clinic immediately. Someone will have to phone and warn that you are on your way (which is a good justification for having a cellular phone!), so that they can be prepared to get your pet on the operating table right away. It is possible for a dog to have more than one incident of gastric torsion, even if he has had his stomach stapled to give extra support.

WAYS TO PREVENT BLOAT
Here are some tips on how to reduce the risk of bloat in your Black Russian Terrier:
- Wait at least an hour after exercising your BRT before feeding him;
- Wait at least two hours after feeding your BRT before exercising him;
- Make sure your BRT is calm, not excited or nervous, at mealtimes;
- Feed high-quality, low-residue diets; avoid those with high cereal content;
- Elevate food and water bowls;
- If your BRT is greedy and eats quickly, reduce the air swallowed by putting something large and inedible in the food bowl so that the dog has to pick around the object and thus eat more slowly;
- Do not allow your BRT to gulp water, especially at mealtime.

Although it is the subject of much research, bloat still manages to take away many dogs before their time and in a very horrible way.

A cross-section through a Black Russian Terrier would show how deep the body cavity is. There are muscles around the vertebrae that give strength to the back and allow it to be flexed and stretched when running. The stomach hangs like a handbag with both straps broken within this deep body cavity.

There also is another way in which the stomach is held in place. There is support provided by the junction with the esophagus or gullet, and there is support provided by the junction with the first part of the small intestine, the "broken straps of the handbag." The only other support is a thin layer of partially opaque "internal skin" called the peritoneum.

It is no wonder that the stomach can move around easily.

Those breeds with the deepest chests are at the greatest risk of having their whole stomachs twist around (gastric torsion). This cuts off the blood supply, prevents the stomach's contents from leaving and increases the amount of gas in the stomach. Once these things have happened, surgery is vital. If the blood supply has been cut off too long and a bit of the stomach wall dies, death of the Black Russian Terrier is almost inevitable.

The horrendous pain of this condition is due to the stomach wall's being stretched by the gas caught in the stomach, as well as the stomach wall's desperately needing the blood that cannot get to it. There is the pain of not being able to pass a much greater than normal amount of wind; added to this is a pain equivalent to that of a heart attack, which is due to the heart muscle's being starved of blood.

A male dog flea,
*Ctenocephalides
canis.*

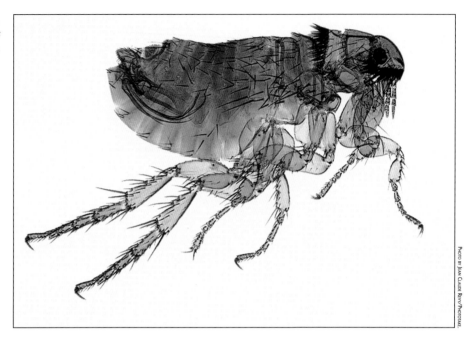

PHOTO BY JEAN CLAUDE REVY/PHOTOTAKE.

EXTERNAL PARASITES

FLEAS

Of all the problems to which dogs are prone, none is more well known and frustrating than fleas. Flea infestation is relatively simple to cure but difficult to prevent. Parasites that are harbored inside the body are a bit more difficult to eradicate but they are easier to control.

To control flea infestation, you have to understand the flea's life cycle. Fleas are often thought of as a summertime problem, but centrally heated homes have changed the patterns and fleas can be found at any time of the year. The most effective method of flea control is a two-stage approach: one stage to kill the adult fleas, and the other to control the development of pre-adult fleas. Unfortunately, no single active ingredient is effective against all stages of the life cycle.

**FLEA KILLER CAUTION—
"POISON"**

Flea-killers are poisonous. You should not spray these toxic chemicals on areas of a dog's body that he licks, including his genitals and his face. Flea killers taken internally are a better answer, but check with your vet in case internal therapy is not advised for your dog.

LIFE CYCLE STAGES

During its life, a flea will pass through four life stages: egg, larva, pupa or nymph and adult. The adult stage is the most visible and irritating stage of the flea life cycle, and this is why the majority of flea-control products concentrate on this stage. The fact is that adult fleas account for only 1% of the total flea population, and the other 99% exist in pre-adult stages, i.e., eggs, larvae and nymphs. The pre-adult stages are barely visible to the naked eye.

THE LIFE CYCLE OF THE FLEA

Eggs are laid on the dog, usually in quantities of about 20 or 30, several times a day. The adult female flea must have a blood meal before each egg-laying session. When first laid, the eggs will cling to the dog's hair, as the eggs are still moist. However, they will quickly dry out and fall from the dog, especially if the dog moves around or scratches. Many eggs will fall off in the dog's favorite area or an area in which he spends a lot of time, such as his bed.

Once the eggs fall from the dog onto the carpet or furniture, they will hatch into larvae. This takes from one to ten days. Larvae are not particularly mobile and will usually travel only a few inches from where they hatch. However, they do have a tendency to move away from bright light and heavy

EN GARDE:
CATCHING FLEAS OFF GUARD!
Consider the following ways to arm yourself against fleas:
• Add a small amount of pennyroyal or eucalyptus oil to your dog's bath. These natural remedies repel fleas.
• Supplement your dog's food with fresh garlic (minced or grated) and a hearty amount of brewer's yeast, both of which ward off fleas.
• Use a flea comb on your dog daily. Submerge fleas in a cup of bleach to kill them quickly.
• Confine the dog to only a few rooms to limit the spread of fleas in the home.
• Vacuum daily...and get all of the crevices! Dispose of the bag every few days until the problem is under control.
• Wash your dog's bedding daily. Cover cushions where your dog sleeps with towels, and wash the towels often.

traffic—under furniture and behind doors are common places to find high quantities of flea larvae.

The flea larvae feed on dead organic matter, including adult flea feces, until they are ready to change into adult fleas. Fleas will usually remain as larvae for around seven days. After this period, the larvae will pupate into protective pupae. While inside the pupae, the larvae will undergo metamorphosis and change into adult fleas. This can take as little time as a few days, but the adult fleas can remain inside the pupae waiting to hatch for up to two years. The pupae are signaled to hatch by certain stimuli, such as physical pressure—the pupae's being stepped on, heat from an animal's lying on the pupae or increased carbon-dioxide levels and vibrations—indicating that a suitable host is available.

Once hatched, the adult flea must feed within a few days. Once the adult flea finds a host, it will not leave voluntarily. It only becomes dislodged by grooming or the host animal's scratching. The adult flea will remain on the

Photo by Dwight R. Kuhl.

host for the duration of its life unless forcibly removed.

TREATING THE ENVIRONMENT AND THE DOG

Treating fleas should be a two-pronged attack. First, the environment needs to be treated; this includes carpets and furniture, especially the dog's bedding and areas underneath furniture. The environment should be treated with a household spray containing an Insect Growth Regulator (IGR) and an insecticide to kill the adult fleas. Most IGRs are effective against eggs and larvae; they actually mimic the fleas' own hormones and stop the eggs and larvae from developing into adult fleas. There are currently no treatments available to attack the pupa stage of the life cycle, so the adult insecticide is used to kill the newly hatched adult fleas before they find a host. Most IGRs are active for many months, while adult insecticides are only active for a few days.

A scanning electron micrograph of a dog or cat flea, *Ctenocephalides*, magnified more than 100x. This image has been colorized for effect.

S. E. M. by Dr Dennis Kunel, University of Hawaii.

THE LIFE CYCLE OF THE FLEA

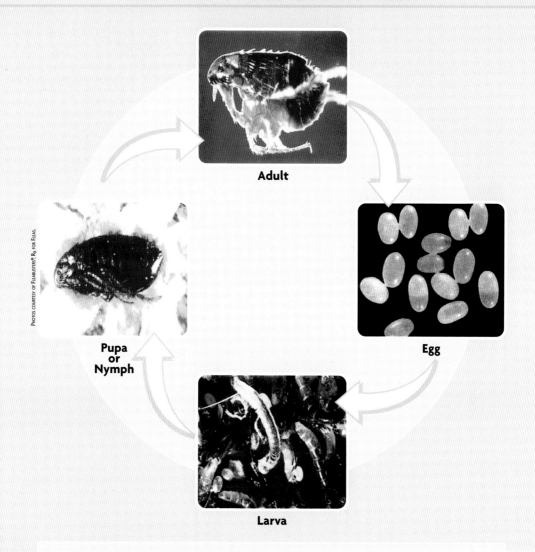

Adult

Egg

Larva

Pupa or Nymph

Fleas have been around for millions of years and have adapted to changing host animals. They are able to go through a complete life cycle in less than one month or they can extend their lives to almost two years by remaining as pupae or cocoons. They do not need blood or any other food for up to 20 months.

INSECT GROWTH REGULATOR (IGR)

Two types of products should be used when treating fleas—a product to treat the pet and a product to treat the home. Adult fleas represent less than 1% of the flea population. The pre-adult fleas (eggs, larvae and pupae) represent more than 99% of the flea population and are found in the environment; it is in the case of pre-adult fleas that products containing an Insect Growth Regulator (IGR) should be used in the home.

IGRs are a new class of compounds used to prevent the development of insects. They do not kill the insect outright, but instead use the insect's biology against it to stop it from completing its growth. Products that contain methoprene are the world's first and leading IGRs. Used to control fleas and other insects, this type of IGR will stop flea larvae from developing and protect the house for up to seven months.

The American dog tick, *Dermacentor variabilis*, is probably the most common tick found on dogs. Look at the strength in its eight legs! No wonder it's hard to detach them.

When treating with a household spray, it is a good idea to vacuum before applying the product. This stimulates as many pupae as possible to hatch into adult fleas. The vacuum cleaner should also be treated with an insecticide to prevent the eggs and larvae that have been collected in the vacuum bag from hatching.

The second stage of treatment is to apply an adult insecticide to the dog. Traditionally, this would be in the form of a collar or a spray, but more recent innovations include digestible insecticides that poison the fleas when they ingest the dog's blood. Alternatively, there are drops that, when placed on the back of the dog's neck, spread throughout the hair and skin to kill adult fleas.

TICKS

Though not as common as fleas, ticks are found all over the tropical and temperate world. They don't bite, like fleas; they harpoon. They dig their sharp proboscis (nose) into the dog's skin and drink the blood. Their only food and drink is dog's blood. Dogs can get Lyme

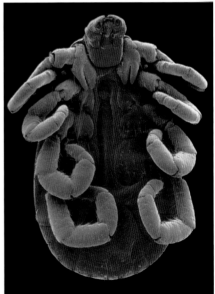

S. E. M. BY DR. DENNIS KUNKEL, UNIVERSITY OF HAWAII

disease, Rocky Mountain spotted fever, tick bite paralysis and many other diseases from ticks. They may live where fleas are found and they like to hide in cracks or seams in walls. They are controlled the same way fleas are controlled.

The American dog tick, *Dermacentor variabilis*, may well be the most common dog tick in many geographical areas, especially those areas where the climate is hot and humid. Most dog ticks have life expectancies of a week to six months, depending upon climatic conditions. They can neither jump nor fly, but they can crawl slowly and can range up to 16 feet to reach a sleeping or unsuspecting dog.

MITES

Just as fleas and ticks can be problematic for your dog, mites can also lead to an itchy nuisance. Microscopic in size, mites are related to ticks and generally take up permanent residence on their host animal—in this case, your dog! The term *mange* refers to any infestation caused by one of the mighty mites, of which there are six varieties that concern dog owners.

Demodex mites cause a condition known as demodicosis (sometimes called red mange or follicular mange), in which the

DEER-TICK CROSSING
The great outdoors may be fun for your dog, but it also is a home to dangerous ticks. Deer ticks carry a bacterium known as *Borrelia burgdorferi* and are most active in the autumn and spring. When infections are caught early, penicillin and tetracycline are effective antibiotics, but, if left untreated, the bacteria may cause neurological, kidney and cardiac problems as well as long-term trouble with walking and painful joints.

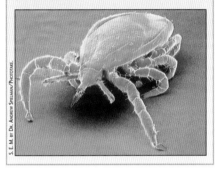

S. E. M. BY DR. ANDREW SPIELMAN/PHOTOTAKE.

PHOTO BY DR. DENNIS KUNKEL, UNIVERSITY OF HAWAII.

The head of an American dog tick, *Dermacentor variabilis*, enlarged and colorized for effect.

The mange mite, *Psoroptes bovis*, can infest cattle and other domestic animals.

PHOTO BY JAMES HAYDEN/YOAV/PHOTOTAKE.

mites live in the dog's hair follicles and sebaceous glands in larger-than-normal numbers. This type of mange is commonly passed from the dam to her puppies and usually shows up on the puppies' muzzles, though demodicosis is not transferable from one normal dog to another. Most dogs recover from this type of mange without any treatment, though topical therapies are commonly prescribed by the vet.

The *Cheyletiellosis* mite is the hook-mouthed culprit associated with "walking dandruff," a condition that affects dogs as well as cats and rabbits. This mite lives on the surface of the animal's skin and is readily transferable through direct or indirect contact with an affected animal. The dandruff is present in the form of scaly skin, which may or may not be itchy. If not treated, this mange can affect a whole kennel of dogs and can be spread to humans as well.

The *Sarcoptes* mite causes intense itching on the dog in the form of a condition known as scabies or sarcoptic mange. The cycle of the *Sarcoptes* mite lasts about three weeks, and the mites live in the top layer of the dog's skin (epidermis), preferably in areas with little hair. Scabies is

Human lice look like dog lice; the two are closely related.

PHOTO BY DWIGHT R. KUHN.

highly contagious and can be passed to humans. Sometimes an allergic reaction to the mite worsens the severe itching associated with sarcoptic mange.

Ear mites, *Otodectes cynotis,* lead to otodectic mange, which most commonly affects the outer ear canal of the dog, though other areas can be affected as well. Dogs with ear-mite infestation commonly scratch at their ears, causing further irritation, and shake their heads. Dark brown droppings in the outer ear confirm the diagnosis. Your vet can prescribe a treatment to flush out the ears and kill any eggs in the ears. A complete month of treatment is necessary to cure the mange.

Two other mites, less common in dogs, include *Dermanyssus gallinae* (the poultry or red mite) and *Eutrombicula alfreddugesi* (the North American mite associated with trombiculidiasis or chigger infestation). The poultry mite frequently lives on chickens, but can transfer to dogs who spend time near farm animals. Chigger infestation affects dogs in the Central US who have exposure to

NOT A DROP TO DRINK
Never allow your dog to swim in polluted water or public areas where water quality can be suspect. Even perfectly clear water can harbor parasites, many of which can cause serious to fatal illnesses in canines. Areas inhabited by waterfowl and other wildlife are especially dangerous.

DO NOT MIX
Never mix parasite-control products without first consulting your vet. Some products can become toxic when combined with others and can cause fatal consequences.

woodlands. The types of mange caused by both of these mites are treatable by vets.

INTERNAL PARASITES
Most animals—fishes, birds and mammals, including dogs and humans—have worms and other parasites that live inside their bodies. According to Dr. Herbert R. Axelrod, the fish pathologist, there are two kinds of parasites: dumb and smart. The smart parasites live in peaceful cooperation with their hosts (symbiosis), while the dumb parasites kill their hosts. Most worm infections are relatively easy to control. If they are not controlled, they weaken the host dog to the point that other medical problems occur, but they do not kill the host as dumb parasites would.

A brown dog tick, *Rhipicephalus sanguineus*, is an uncommon but annoying tick found on dogs.
PHOTO BY CAROLINA BIOLOGICAL SUPPLY/PHOTOTAKE.

PHOTO BY CAROLINA BIOLOGICAL SUPPLY/PHOTOTAKE.

The roundworm *Rhabditis* can infect both dogs and humans.

ROUNDWORMS

Average-size dogs can pass 1,360,000 roundworm eggs every day. For example, if there were only 1 million dogs in the world, the world would be saturated with thousands of tons of dog feces. These feces would contain around 15,000,000,000 roundworm eggs.

Up to 31% of home yards and children's sand boxes in the US contain roundworm eggs.

Flushing dog's feces down the toilet is not a safe practice because the usual sewage treatments do not destroy roundworm eggs.

Infected puppies start shedding roundworm eggs at three weeks of age. They can be infected by their mother's milk.

The roundworm, *Ascaris lumbricoides.*

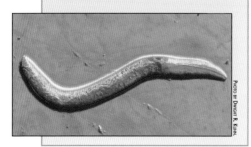

PHOTO BY DWIGHT R. KUHN.

ROUNDWORMS

The roundworms that infect dogs are known scientifically as *Toxocara canis.* They live in the dog's intestines and shed eggs continually. It has been estimated that a dog produces about 6 or more ounces of feces every day. Each ounce of feces averages hundreds of thousands of roundworm eggs. There are no known areas in which dogs roam that do not contain roundworm eggs. The greatest danger of roundworms is that they infect people, too! It is wise to have your dog tested regularly for roundworms.

In young puppies, roundworms cause bloated bellies, diarrhea, coughing and vomiting, and are transmitted from the dam (through blood or milk). Affected puppies will not appear as animated as normal puppies. The worms appear spaghetti-like, measuring as long as 6 inches. Adult dogs can acquire roundworms through coprophagia (eating contaminated feces) or by killing rodents that carry roundworms.

Roundworm infection can kill puppies and cause severe problems in adults, as the hatched larvae travel to the lungs and trachea through the bloodstream. Cleanliness is the best preventative for roundworms. Always pick up after your dog and dispose of feces in appropriate receptacles.

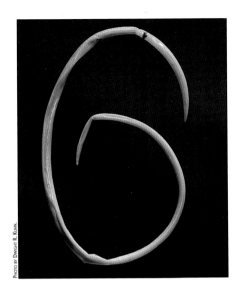

HOOKWORMS

In the United States, dog owners have to be concerned about four different species of hookworm, the most common and most serious of which is *Ancylostoma caninum,* which prefers warm climates. The others are *Ancylostoma braziliense, Ancylostoma tubaeforme* and *Uncinaria stenocephala,* the latter of which is a concern to dogs living in the Northern US and Canada, as this species prefers cold climates. Hookworms are dangerous to humans as well as to dogs and cats, and can be the cause of severe anemia due to iron deficiency. The worm uses its teeth to attach itself to the dog's intestines and changes the site of its attachment about six times per day. Each time the worm

repositions itself, the dog loses blood and can become anemic. *Ancylostoma caninum* is the most likely of the four species to cause anemia in the dog.

Symptoms of hookworm infection include dark stools, weight loss, general weakness, pale coloration and anemia, as well as possible skin problems. Fortunately, hookworms are easily purged from the affected dog with a number of medications that have proven effective. Discuss these with your vet. Most heartworm preventatives include a hookworm insecticide as well.

Owners also must be aware that hookworms can infect humans, who can acquire the larvae through exposure to contaminated feces. Since the worms cannot complete their life cycle on a human, the worms simply infest the skin and cause irritation. This condition is known as cutaneous larva migrans syndrome. As a preventative, use disposable gloves or a "poop-scoop" to pick up your dog's droppings and prevent your dog (or neighborhood cats) from defecating in children's play areas.

The hookworm, *Ancylostoma caninum.*

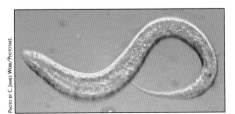

The infective stage of the hookworm larva.

TAPEWORMS

Humans, rats, squirrels, foxes, coyotes, wolves and domestic dogs are all susceptible to tapeworm infection. Except in humans, tapeworms are usually not a fatal infection. Infected individuals can harbor 1000 parasitic worms.

Tapeworms, like some other types of worm, are hermaphroditic, meaning male and female in the same worm.

If dogs eat infected rats or mice, or anything else infected with tapeworm, they get the tapeworm disease. One month after attaching to a dog's intestine, the worm starts shedding eggs. These eggs are infective immediately. Infective eggs can live for a few months without a host animal.

The head and rostellum (the round prominence on the scolex) of a tapeworm, which infects dogs and humans.

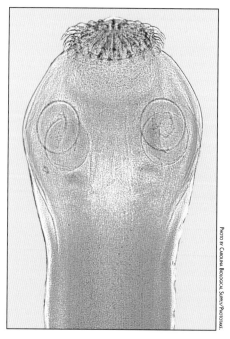

PHOTO BY CAROLINA BIOLOGICAL SUPPLY/PHOTOTAKE.

TAPEWORMS

There are many species of tapeworm, all of which are carried by fleas! The most common tapeworm affecting dogs is known as *Dipylidium caninum*. The dog eats the flea and starts the tapeworm cycle. Humans can also be infected with tapeworms—so don't eat fleas! Fleas are so small that your dog could pass them onto your hands, your plate or your food and thus make it possible for you to ingest a flea that is carrying tapeworm eggs.

While tapeworm infection is not life-threatening in dogs (smart parasite!), it can be the cause of a very serious liver disease for humans. About 50% of the humans infected with *Echinococcus multilocularis*, a type of tapeworm that causes alveolar hydatid, perish.

WHIPWORMS

In North America, whipworms are counted among the most common parasitic worms in dogs. The whipworm's scientific name is *Trichuris vulpis*. These worms attach themselves in the lower parts of the intestine, where they feed. Affected dogs may only experience upset tummies, colic and diarrhea. These worms, however, can live for months or years in the dog, beginning their larval stage in the small intestine, spending their adult stage in the large intestine and finally passing infective eggs through the dog's feces. The only way to detect whipworms is through a fecal examination, though this is not always foolproof. Treatment for whipworms is tricky, due to the worms' unusual life-cycle pattern, and very often dogs are reinfected due to exposure to infective eggs on the ground. The whipworm eggs can survive in the environment for as long as five years; thus, cleaning up droppings in your own backyard as well as in public places is absolutely essential for sanitation purposes and the health of your dog and others.

THREADWORMS
Though less common than round-worms, hookworms and those previously mentioned, thread-worms concern dog owners in the Southwestern US and Gulf Coast area where the climate is hot and humid. Living in the small intestine of the dog, this worm measures a mere 2 millimeters and is round in shape. Like that of the whipworm, the threadworm's life cycle is very complex and the eggs and larvae are passed through the feces. A deadly disease in humans, *Strongyloides* readily infects people, and the handling of feces is the most common means of transmission. Threadworms are most often seen in young puppies; bloody diarrhea and pneumonia are symptoms. Sick puppies must be isolated and treated immediately; vets recommend a follow-up treatment one month later.

HEARTWORM PREVENTATIVES

There are many heartworm preventatives on the market, many of which are sold at your veterinarian's office. These products can be given daily or monthly, depending on the manufacturer's instructions. All of these preventatives contain chemical insecticides directed at killing heartworms, which leads to some controversy among dog owners. In effect, heartworm preventatives are necessary evils, though you should determine how necessary based on your pet's lifestyle. There is no doubt that heartworm is a dreadful disease that threatens the lives of dogs. However, the likelihood of your dog's being bitten by an infected mosquito is slim in most places, and a mosquito-repellent (or an herbal remedy such as Wormwood or Black Walnut) is much safer for your dog and will not compromise his immune system (the way heartworm preventatives will). Should you decide to use the traditional preventative "medications," you can consider giving the pill every other or third month. Since the toxins in the pill will kill the heartworms at all stages of development, the pill would be effective in killing larvae, nymphs or adults and it takes four months for the larvae to reach the adult stage. Thus, there is no rationale to poisoning the dog's system on a monthly basis. Lastly, do not give the pill during the winter months, since there are no mosquitoes around to pass on their infection, unless you live in a tropical environment.

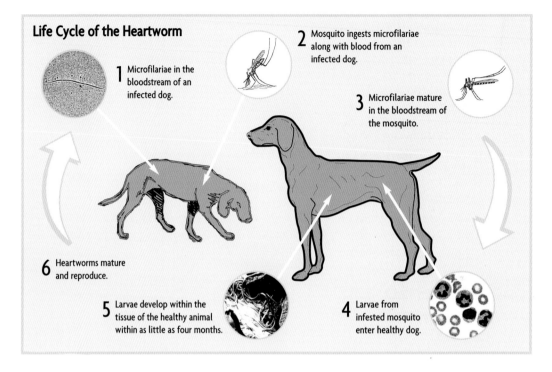

Life Cycle of the Heartworm

1 Microfilariae in the bloodstream of an infected dog.

2 Mosquito ingests microfilariae along with blood from an infected dog.

3 Microfilariae mature in the bloodstream of the mosquito.

4 Larvae from infested mosquito enter healthy dog.

5 Larvae develop within the tissue of the healthy animal within as little as four months.

6 Heartworms mature and reproduce.

HEARTWORMS

Heartworms are thin, extended worms up to 12 inches long, which live in a dog's heart and the major blood vessels surrounding it. Dogs may have up to 200 worms. Symptoms may be loss of energy, loss of appetite, coughing, the development of a pot belly and anemia.

Heartworms are transmitted by mosquitoes. The mosquito drinks the blood of an infected dog and takes in larvae with the blood. The larvae, called microfilariae, develop within the body of the mosquito and are passed on to the next dog bitten after the larvae mature. It takes two to three weeks for the larvae to develop to the infective stage within the body of the mosquito. Dogs are usually treated at about six weeks of age and maintained on a prophylactic dose given monthly.

Blood testing for heartworms is not necessarily indicative of how seriously your dog is infected. Although this is a dangerous disease, it is not easy for a dog to be infected. Discuss the various preventatives with your vet, as there are many different types now available. Together you can decide on a safe course of prevention for your dog.

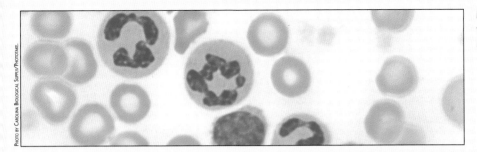

Magnified heartworm larvae, *Dirofilaria immitis.*

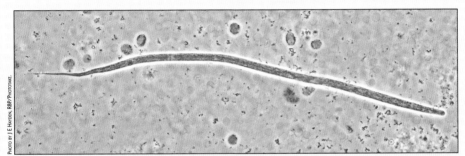

Heartworm, *Dirofilaria immitis.*

The heart of a dog infected with canine heartworm, *Dirofilaria immitis.*

BLACK RUSSIAN TERRIER

To the novice, exhibiting a Black Russian Terrier in the show ring may look easy, but it takes a lot of hard work and devotion to do top winning at conformation shows, not to mention a little luck, too! The first concept that the canine novice learns when watching a dog show is that each dog first competes against members of his own breed. Once the judge has selected the best member of each breed (Best of Breed), provided that the show is judged on a Group system, that chosen dog will compete with other dogs in his group. Finally, the dogs chosen first in each group will compete for Best in Show.

The second concept that you must understand is that the dogs are not actually compared against one another. The judge compares each dog against his breed standard. While some early breed standards were indeed based on specific dogs that were famous or popular, many dedicated enthusiasts say that a perfect specimen, as described in the standard, has never walked into a show ring, has never been bred and, to the woe of dog breeders around the globe, does

not exist. Breeders attempt to get as close to this ideal as possible with every litter, but theoretically the "perfect" dog is so elusive that it is impossible. (And if the "perfect" dog were born, breeders and judges would never agree that it was indeed "perfect.")

If you are interested in exploring the world of dog showing, your best bet is to join your local or national breed club, i.e., the Black Russian Terrier Club of America. These clubs often host both regional and national specialties, shows only for Black Russians, which can include conformation as well as agility or obedience trials. Even if you have no intention of competing with your Blackie, a specialty is like a festival for lovers of the breed who congregate to share their favorite topic: Black Russian Terriers! Clubs also send out newsletters, and some organize training days and seminars in order that people may learn more about their chosen breed. To locate the breed club closest to you, contact the American Kennel Club or the club with which your BRT is registered.

If your Black Russian is of age and registered, you can enter him in a dog show where the breed is offered classes. Only unaltered dogs can be entered in a dog show, so if you have spayed or neutered your Black Russian Terrier, you cannot compete in conformation shows. The reason for this is simple. Dog shows are the main forum to prove which representatives in a breed are worthy of being bred. Only dogs that have achieved championships—the recognized "seal of approval" for quality in pure-bred dogs—should be bred. Altered dogs, however, can participate in other events such as obedience trials and the Canine Good Citizen program.

Before you actually step into the ring, you would be well advised to sit back and observe the judge's ring procedure. If it is your first time in the ring, do not be over-anxious and run to the front of the line. It is much better to stand back and study how the exhibitor in front of you is performing.

The judge asks each handler to "stack" the dog, hopefully showing the dog off to his best advantage. The judge will observe the dog from a distance and from different angles, and approach the dog to check his teeth, overall structure, alertness and muscle tone, as well as consider how well the dog "conforms" to the standard. Most importantly, the judge will have the exhibitor move the dog around the ring in some pattern that he should specify (another advantage to not going first,

CLUB CONTACTS:
You can get information about dog shows from national kennel clubs:

American Kennel Club
5580 Centerview Dr., Raleigh, NC 27606-3390
www.akc.org

United Kennel Club
100 E. Kilgore Road, Kalamazoo, MI 49002
www.ukcdogs.com

Canadian Kennel Club
89 Skyway Ave., Suite 100, Etobicoke, Ontario M9W 6R4, Canada
www.ckc.ca

The Kennel Club
1-5 Clarges St., Piccadilly, London W1Y 8AB, UK
www.the-kennel-club.org.uk

Fédération Cynologique Internationale
14, rue Leopold II, B-6530 Thuin, Belgium
www.fci.be

but always listen since some judges change their directions—and the judge is always right!). Finally, the judge will give the dog one last look before moving on to the next exhibitor.

If you are not in the top four in your class at your first show, do not be discouraged. Be patient and consistent, and you may eventually find yourself in a winning line-up. Remember that the winners were once in your shoes and have devoted many hours and much money to earn the placement. If you find that your dog is losing every time and never getting a nod, it may be time to consider a different dog sport or just to enjoy your Black Russian Terrier as a pet. Parent clubs offer other events, such as agility, tracking, obedience, Schutzhund and more, which may be of interest to the owner of a well-trained Black Russian Terrier.

OBEDIENCE TRIALS
Obedience trials in the US trace back to the early 1930s when organized obedience training was developed to demonstrate how well dog and owner could work together. The pioneer of obedience trials is Mrs. Helen Whitehouse Walker, a Standard Poodle fancier, who designed a series of exercises after the Associated Sheep, Police Army Dog Society of Great Britain. Since the days of Mrs. Walker, obedience trials have grown by leaps and bounds, and today there are over 2,000 trials with more than 100,000 dogs competing each year, and that's in the US alone! Any registered dog can enter an obedience trial, regardless of conformational disqualifications or neutering.

Obedience trials are divided into three levels of progressive difficulty. At the first level, the Novice, dogs compete for the title Companion Dog (CD); at the intermediate level, the Open, dogs compete for the title Companion Dog Excellent (CDX); and at the advanced level, the Utility, dogs compete for the title Utility Dog (UD). Classes are sub-divided into "A" (for beginners) and "B" (for

more experienced handlers). A perfect score at any level is 200, and a dog must score 170 or better to earn a "leg," of which three are needed to earn the title. To earn points, the dog must score more than 50% of the available points in each exercise; the possible points range from 20 to 40.

Once a dog has earned the UD title, he can compete with other proven obedience dogs for the coveted title of Utility Dog Excellent (UDX), which requires that the dog win "legs" in ten shows. Utility Dogs who earn "legs" in Open B and Utility B earn points toward their Obedience Trial Champion title. In 1977, the title Obedience Trial Champion (OTCh.) was established by the AKC. To become an OTCh., a dog needs to earn 100 points, which requires three first places in Open B and Utility under three different judges.

AGILITY TRIALS
Having had its origins in the UK back in 1977, AKC agility had its official beginning in the US in August 1994, when the first licensed agility trials were held. The AKC allows all registered breeds (including Miscellaneous Class breeds) to participate, providing the dog is 12 months of age or older. Agility is designed so that the handler demonstrates how well the dog can work at his side. The handler directs his dog over an obstacle course that includes jumps (such as those used

in working or obedience trials), as well as tires, the dog walk, weave poles, pipe tunnels, collapsed tunnels, etc. While working his way through the course, the dog must keep one eye and ear on the handler and the rest of his body on the course. The handler gives verbal and hand signals to guide the dog through the course.

The first organization to promote agility trials in the US was the United States Dog Agility Association, Inc. (USDAA), which was established in 1986 and spawned numerous member clubs around the country. Both the USDAA and the AKC offer titles to winning dogs.

Agility is great fun for dog and owner in countries worldwide, with many rewards for everyone involved. Interested owners should join a training club that has obstacles and experienced agility handlers who can introduce you and your dog to the "ropes" (and tires, tunnels, etc.).

WORKING TRIALS

The agile Black Russian Terrier is an excellent candidate for working trials in countries that offer such venues to prove a dog's worth as a working dog and partner. Working trials provide an energetic outlet for

This team of Black Russian Terriers was awarded Best Group in Show.

any Blackie who has had some measure of obedience training and who enjoys a higher level of physical activity.

In working trials, the dogs compete against a standard of performance rather than each other. The degree of difficulty increases with each working class. The tests combine exercises in obedience (heeling on- and off-leash and the send-away; static exercises of sit and down), agility tests of jumping, scaling and recalls, retrieving exercises and nosework, including the search and tracking of articles. Dogs must earn at least 70% in their group in order to qualify and earn the corresponding certificate.

TRACKING
Any dog is capable of tracking, using his nose to follow a trail. Tracking tests are exciting and competitive ways to test your BRT's ability to search and rescue. The AKC started tracking tests in 1937, when the first AKC-licensed test took place as part of an obedience trial. Ten years later in 1947, the AKC offered the first title, Tracking Dog (TD). It was not until 1980 that the AKC added the Tracking Dog Excellent (TDX) title, which was followed by the Versatile Surface Tracking (VST) title in 1995. The title Champion Tracker (CT) is awarded to a dog who has earned all three titles.

In the beginning level of tracking, the owner follows the dog through a field on a long leash. To earn the TD title, the dog must follow a track laid by a human 30 to 120 minutes prior. The track is about 500 yards long with up to 5 directional changes. The TDX requires that the dog follow a track that is 3 to 5 hours old over a course up to 1,000 yards long with up to 7 directional changes. The VST requires that the dog follow a track up to 5 hours old through an urban setting.

FÉDÉRATION CYNOLOGIQUE INTERNATIONALE
Established in 1911, the Fédération Cynologique Internationale (FCI) represents the "world kennel club." This international body brings uniformity to the breeding, judging and showing of pure-bred dogs. Although the FCI originally included only five European nations: France, Germany, Austria, the Netherlands and Belgium (which remains its headquarters), the organization today embraces nations on six continents and recognizes well over 300 breeds of pure-bred dog.

The FCI sponsors both national and international shows. The hosting country determines the judging system and breed standards are always based on the breed's country of origin. Dogs from every country can participate in these impressive canine spectacles, the largest of which is the World Dog Show, which is hosted in a different country each year.

Black Russian Terrier breed judging at an FCI show. The breed attracts many spectators, as evidenced by the crowd of excited onlookers outside the ring, waiting to see who will be crowned Best of Breed.

There are three titles attainable through the FCI: the International Champion, which is the most prestigious; the International Beauty Champion, which is based on aptitude certificates in different countries; and the International Trial Champion, which is based on achievement in obedience trials in different countries. An FCI title requires a dog to win three CACs (*Certificats d'Aptitude au Championnat*) at regional or club shows under three different judges who are breed specialists. The title of International Champion is gained by winning four CACIBs (*Certificats d'Aptitude au Championnat International de Beauté*), which are offered only at international shows, with at least a one-year lapse between the first and fourth award.

The FCI is divided into ten groups, and the BRT competes in Group 2 (for Working Dogs) except in France where it competes in Group 3 (for Terriers). At the World Dog Show, the following classes are offered for each breed: Puppy Class (6–9 months), Junior Class (9–18 months), Open Class (15 months or older) and Champion Class. A dog can be awarded a classification of Excellent, Very Good, Good, Sufficient and Not Sufficient. Puppies can be awarded classifications of Very Promising, Promising or Not Promising. Four placements are made in each class. After all classes are judged, a Best of Breed is selected. Other special groups and classes may also be shown. Each exhibitor showing a dog receives a written evaluation from the judge.

Besides the World Dog Show and other all-breed shows, you can exhibit your dog at specialty shows held by different breed clubs. Specialty shows may have their own regulations.

BEHAVIOR OF YOUR
BLACK RUSSIAN TERRIER

THINK LIKE A DOG

Dogs do not think like humans, nor do humans think like dogs, though we try. Unfortunately, a dog is incapable of comprehending how humans think, so the responsibility falls on the owner to adopt a viable canine mindset. Dogs cannot rationalize, and they exist in the present moment. Many a dog owner makes the mistake in training of thinking that he can reprimand his dog for something the dog did a while ago. Basically, you cannot even reprimand a dog for something he did 20 seconds ago! Either catch him in the act or forget it! It is a waste of your and your dog's time—in his mind, you are reprimanding him for whatever he is doing at that moment.

Discuss bad habits with your vet and he can recommend a behavioral specialist to consult when appropriate. Since behavioral abnormalities are the main reason that owners abandon their pets, we hope that you will make a valiant effort to solve your BRT's problems. Patience and understanding are virtues that must dwell in every pet-loving household.

AGGRESSION

This is a problem that concerns all responsible owners of dogs of any breed. Aggression can be a very big problem in dogs, and, when not controlled, always becomes dangerous. An aggressive dog, no matter the size, may lunge at, bite or even attack a person or another dog. Aggressive behavior is not to be tolerated. It is more than just inappropriate behavior; it is painful for a family to watch their dog become unpredictable in his behavior to the point where they are afraid of him. While not all aggressive behavior is dangerous, growling, baring teeth and so forth can be frightening. It is important to ascertain why the dog is acting in this manner. Aggression is a display of dominance, and the dog should not have the dominant role in his pack, which is, in this case, your family.

It is important not to challenge an aggressive dog, as this could provoke an attack. Observe your Black Russian Terrier's body language. Does he make direct eye contact and stare? Does he try to make himself as large as possible: ears pricked, chest out, tail erect? Height and size signify authority in a dog pack—being taller or "above" another dog literally means that he is "above" in social status. These body signals tell you that your Black Russian Terrier thinks he is in charge, a problem that needs to be addressed. An aggressive dog is unpredictable; you never know when he is going to strike and what he is going to do. You cannot understand why a dog that is playful one minute is growling the next.

Fear is a common cause of aggression in dogs. Perhaps your Black Russian Terrier had a negative experience as a puppy, which causes him to be fearful when a similar situation presents itself later in life. The dog may act aggressively in order to protect himself from whatever is making him afraid. It is not always easy to determine what is making your dog fearful, but if you can isolate what brings out the fear reaction, you can help the dog get over it.

Supervise your Black Russian Terrier's interactions with people and other dogs, and praise the dog when it goes well. If he starts to act aggressively in a situation, correct him and remove him from the situation. Do not let people approach the dog and start petting him without your express permission. That way, you can have the dog sit to accept petting, and praise him when he behaves

A little play-fighting among comrades is nothing to worry about!

properly. You are focusing on praise and on modifying his behavior by rewarding him when he acts appropriately. By being gentle and by supervising his interactions, you are showing him that there is no need to be afraid or defensive.

The best solution is to consult a behavioral specialist, one who has experience with the breed or similar breeds. Together, perhaps you can pinpoint the cause of your dog's aggression and do something about it. An aggressive dog cannot be trusted, and a dog that cannot be trusted is not safe to have as a family pet. If, very unusually, you find that your pet has become untrustworthy and you feel it necessary to seek a new home with a more suitable family and environment, explain fully to the new owners all of your reasons for rehoming the dog to be fair to all concerned. In the *very worst* case, if the dog is truly dangerous, you will have to consider euthanasia.

AGGRESSION TOWARD OTHER DOGS

A dog's aggressive behavior toward another dog stems from not enough exposure to other dogs at an early age. If other dogs make your Black Russian Terrier nervous and agitated, he will lash out as a protective mechanism. A dog that has not received sufficient exposure to other canines tends to think that he is the only dog on the planet. The animal becomes so dominant that he does not even show signs that he is fearful or threatened. Without growling or any other physical signal as a warning, he will lunge at and bite the other dog. Male BRTs do tend to be dominant, which can lead to dog-aggression, but Blackies are usually not the ones to make the first move.

A way to correct aggression toward other dogs is to let your Black Russian Terrier approach another dog when walking on lead. Watch very closely and, at the first sign of aggression, correct your Black Russian Terrier and pull him away. Scold him for any sign of discomfort, and then praise him when he ignores the other dog. Keep this up until either he stops the aggressive behavior, learns to ignore other dogs or even accepts other dogs. Praise him lavishly for his correct behavior.

DOMINANT AGGRESSION

A social hierarchy is firmly established in a wild dog pack. The dog wants to dominate those under him and please those above him. Dogs know that there must be a leader. If you are not the obvious choice for czar, the dog will assume the throne! These conflicting innate desires are what a dog owner is up against when he sets about training a dog. In training a dog to obey commands, the owner is reinforcing that he is the top dog in the "pack" and that the dog should, and should want to, serve his superior. Thus, the owner is suppressing the dog's urge to dominate by modifying his behavior and making him obedient.

DOMINANT AGGRESSION
Never allow your puppy to growl at you or bare his tiny teeth. Such behavior is dominant and aggressive. If not corrected, the dog will repeat the behavior, which will become more threatening as he grows larger and will eventually lead to biting.

An important part of training is taking every opportunity to reinforce that you are the leader. It is a constant effort to show the dog that his place in the pack is at the bottom. This is not meant to sound cruel or inhumane. You love your Black Russian Terrier and you should treat him with care and affection. You likely did not get a dog just so you could control another creature. Dog training is not about being cruel, it is about molding the dog's behavior into what is acceptable and teaching him to live by your rules. In theory, it is quite simple: catch him in appropriate behavior and reward him for it. Add a dog into the equation and it becomes a bit more trying, but, as a rule of thumb, positive reinforcement is what works best.

With a dominant dog, punishment and negative reinforcement can have the opposite effect of what you are after. It can make a dog fearful and/or act out aggressively if he feels he is being challenged. Remember, a dominant dog perceives himself at the top of the social heap and will fight to defend his perceived status. The best way to prevent that is to never give him reason to think that he is in control in the first place.

If you are having trouble training your Black Russian Terrier and it seems as if he is constantly challenging your authority, seek the help of an obedience trainer or behavioral specialist. A professional will work with both you and your dog to teach you effective techniques to use at home. Beware of trainers who rely on excessively harsh methods; scolding is necessary now and then, but the focus in your training should *always* be on positive reinforcement.

SEPARATION ANXIETY
Recognized by behaviorists as the most common form of stress for dogs, separation anxiety can also lead to destructive behaviors in your dog. It's more than your Black Russian Terrier's howling his displeasure at your leaving the house and his being left alone. This is a normal reaction, no different than the child who cries as his mother leaves him on the first day at school. Separation anxiety is more serious. In fact, if you are constantly with your dog, he will come to expect you with him all of the time, making it even more traumatic for him when you are not there.

Obviously, you enjoy spending time with your dog, and he thrives on your love and attention. However, it should not become a dependent relationship in which he is heartbroken without you. This broken heart can also bring on destructive behavior as well as loss of appetite, depression and lack of interest in play and interaction. Canine behaviorists have been spending much time and energy to help owners better understand the significance of this stressful condition.

One thing you can do to minimize separation anxiety is to make your entrances and exits as low-key as possible. Do not give your dog a long drawn-out goodbye, and do not lavish him with hugs and kisses when you return. This is giving in to the attention that he craves, and it will only make him miss it more when you are away. Another thing you can try is to give your dog a treat when you leave; this will not only keep him occupied and keep his mind off the fact that you have just left, but it will also help him associate your leaving with a pleasant experience.

You may have to accustom your dog to being left alone at intervals. Of course, when your dog starts whimpering as you approach the door, your first instinct will be to run to him and comfort him, but do not do it! Eventually he will adjust to your absence. His anxiety stems from being placed in an unfamiliar situation; by familiarizing him with being alone, he will learn that he will survive. That is not to say you should purposely leave your dog home alone, but the dog needs to know that, while he can depend on you for his care, you do not have to be by his side 24 hours a day. Some behaviorists recommend tiring the dog out before you leave home—take him for a good long walk or engage in a game of fetch.

When the dog is alone in the house, he should be placed in his crate—another distinct advantage to crate-training your dog. The crate should be placed in his familiar happy family area, where he normally sleeps and already feels comfortable, thereby making him feel more at ease when he is alone. Be sure to give the dog a special chew toy to enjoy while he settles into his crate.

A canine companion can help ease a dog's loneliness, but it's no substitute for a strong bond and time spent with his owner.

SEXUAL BEHAVIOR

Dogs exhibit certain sexual behaviors that may have influenced your choice of male or female when you first purchased your Black Russian Terrier. To a certain extent, spaying/neutering will eliminate these behaviors, but if you are purchasing a dog that you wish to breed from, you should be aware of what you will have to deal with throughout the dog's life.

Female dogs usually have two estruses per year, with each season lasting about three weeks. These are the only times in which a female dog will mate, and she usually will not allow this until the second week of the cycle, although this varies from bitch to bitch. If not bred during the heat cycle, it is not uncommon for a bitch to experience a false pregnancy, in which her mammary glands swell and she exhibits maternal tendencies toward toys or other objects.

With male dogs, owners must be aware that whole dogs (dogs who are not neutered) have the natural inclination to mark their territory. Males mark their territory by spraying small amounts of urine as they lift their legs in a macho ritual. Marking can occur both outdoors in the yard and around the neighborhood as well as indoors on furniture legs, curtains and the sofa. Such behavior can be very frustrating

for the owner; early training is strongly urged before the "urge" strikes your dog. Neutering the male at an appropriate early age can solve this problem before it becomes a habit.

Other problems associated with males are wandering and mounting. Both of these habits, of course, belong to the unneutered dog, whose sexual drive leads him away from home in search of the bitch in heat. Males will mount females in heat, as well as any other dog, male or female, that happens to catch their fancy. Other possible mounting partners include his owner, the furniture, guests to the home and strangers on the street. Discourage such behavior early on.

Owners must further recognize that mounting is not merely a sexual expression but also one of dominance, seen in males and females alike. Be consistent and be persistent, and you will find that you can "move mounters."

CHEWING

The national canine pastime is chewing! Every dog loves to sink his "canines" into a tasty bone, so it is important to provide your dog with appropriate chew toys so that he doesn't destroy your possessions or make a habit of gnawing on your hands and fingers. Dogs need to chew to massage their gums, to make their new teeth feel better and to exercise their jaws. This is a natural behavior that is deeply embedded in all things canine. Your role as owner is not to stop the dog's chewing, but rather to redirect it to positive, chew-worthy objects. Be an informed owner and purchase proper chew toys for your Blackie, like strong nylon bones made for large dogs that will not splinter. BRTs need sturdy, strong toys, so be sure that the toys you offer to your Blackie are safe and durable, since your dog's safety is at risk. Again, the owner is responsible for ensuring a dog-proof environment.

The best answer is prevention; that is, put your shoes, handbags and other tasty objects in their proper places (out of the reach of the growing canine mouth). Direct your puppy to his toys whenever you see him "tasting" the furniture legs or the leg of your jeans. Make a loud noise to attract the pup's attention and immediately escort him to his chew toy and engage him with the toy for at least four minutes, praising and encouraging him all the while. An array of safe, interesting chew toys will keep your dog's mind and teeth occupied, and distracted from chewing on things he shouldn't.

Some trainers recommend deterrents, such as hot pepper, a bitter spice or a product designed for this purpose, to discourage the dog from chewing on unwanted objects. Test these products to see which works best before investing in large quantities.

JUMPING UP

Jumping up is a dog's friendly way of saying hello! Some dog owners do not mind when their dog jumps up. The problem arises when guests come to the house and the dog greets them in the same manner—whether they like it or not! However friendly the greeting may be, the chances are that your visitors will not appreciate your dog's enthusiasm, especially with a dog the size of the Black Russian. The dog will not be able to distinguish upon whom he can jump and whom he cannot. Therefore, it is probably best to discourage this behavior entirely.

Pick a command such as "Off" (avoid using "Down" since you will use that for the dog to lie down) and tell him "Off" when he jumps up. Place him on the

---

NO JUMPING
Stop a dog from jumping up before he jumps. If he is getting ready to jump onto you, simply walk away. If he jumps up on you before you can turn away, lift your knee so that it bumps him in the chest. Do not be forceful. Your dog soon will realize that jumping up is not a productive way of getting attention.

ground on all fours and have him sit, praising him the whole time. Always lavish him with praise and petting when he is in the sit position. In this way, you can give him a warm affectionate greeting, let him know that you are as pleased to see him as he is to see you and instill good manners at the same time!

DIGGING

Digging, which is seen as destructive behavior to humans, is actually quite a natural behavior in dogs. Terriers (the "earth dogs") are most associated with the digging, and although the Blackie is not your typical terrier, he can be a digger. Any dog's desire to dig can be irrepressible and most frustrating to his owners.

When digging occurs in your yard, it is actually a normal behavior redirected into something the dog can do in his everyday life. In the wild, a dog would be actively seeking food, making his own shelter, etc. He would be using his paws in a purposeful manner for his survival. Since you provide him with food and shelter, he has no need to use his paws for these purposes, and so the energy that he would be using may manifest itself in the form of craters all over your yard and in your flower beds.

Perhaps your dog is digging as a reaction to boredom—it is

Don't overlook the "terrier" in your Black Russian Terrier's name; when it comes to digging, he will relish the opportunity to get his paws dirty.

somewhat similar to someone's eating a whole bag of chips in front of the TV—because they are there and there is nothing better to do! Basically, the answer is to provide the dog with adequate play and exercise so that his mind and paws are occupied, and so that he feels as if he is doing something useful.

Of course, digging is easiest to control if it is stopped as soon as possible, but it is often hard to catch a dog in the act. If your dog is a compulsive digger and is not easily distracted by other activities, you can designate an area on your property where he is allowed to dig. If you catch him digging in an off-limits area of the yard, immediately take him to the approved area and praise him for digging there. Keep a close eye on him so that you can catch him in the act—that is the only way to make him understand what is permitted and what is not. If you take him to a hole he dug an hour ago and tell him "No," he will understand that you are not fond of holes, dirt or flowers. If you catch him while he is stifle-deep in your tulips, that is when he will get your message.

BARKING

Dogs cannot talk—oh, what they would say if they could! Instead, barking is a dog's way of "talking." It can be somewhat frustrating because it is not always easy to tell what a dog means by his bark—is he excited, happy, frightened or angry? Whatever it is that the dog is trying to say, he should not be punished for barking. It is only when the barking becomes excessive, and when the excessive barking becomes a bad habit, that the behavior needs to be modified.

The BRT is a big dog that can produce a bark befitting of his size, but he is not especially vocal unless there is necessity to be so. For example, if an intruder came into your home in the

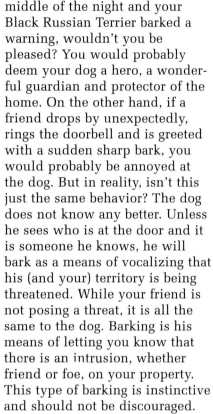

middle of the night and your Black Russian Terrier barked a warning, wouldn't you be pleased? You would probably deem your dog a hero, a wonderful guardian and protector of the home. On the other hand, if a friend drops by unexpectedly, rings the doorbell and is greeted with a sudden sharp bark, you would probably be annoyed at the dog. But in reality, isn't this just the same behavior? The dog does not know any better. Unless he sees who is at the door and it is someone he knows, he will bark as a means of vocalizing that his (and your) territory is being threatened. While your friend is not posing a threat, it is all the same to the dog. Barking is his means of letting you know that there is an intrusion, whether friend or foe, on your property. This type of barking is instinctive and should not be discouraged.

Excessive habitual barking, however, is a problem that should be corrected early on. As your Black Russian Terrier grows up, you will be able to tell when his barking is purposeful and when it is for no reason. You will become able to distinguish your dog's different barks and their meanings. For example, the bark when someone comes to the door will be different than the bark when he is excited to see you. It is similar to a person's tone of voice, except that the dog has to rely

BARKING STANCE

Did you know that a dog is less likely to bark when sitting than standing? Watch your dog the next time that you suspect he is about to start barking. You'll notice that as he does, he gets up on all four feet. Hence, when teaching a dog to stop barking, it helps to get him to sit before you command him to be quiet.

totally on tone of voice because he does not have the benefit of using words. An incessant barker will be evident at an early age.

There are some things that encourage a dog to bark. For example, if your dog barks non-stop for a few minutes and you give him a treat to quiet him, he believes that you are rewarding him for barking. He will associate barking with getting a treat and will keep doing it until he is rewarded. On the other hand, if you give him a command such as "Quiet" and praise him after he has stopped barking for a few seconds, he will get the idea that being "quiet" is what you want him to do.

FOOD STEALING
Is your dog devising ways of stealing food from your coffee table or kitchen counter? If so, you must answer the following questions: Is your Black Russian Terrier a bit hungry, or is he "constantly famished" like many dogs seem to be? Face it, some dogs are more food-motivated than others. They are totally obsessed by the smell of food and can only think of their next meal. Food stealing is terrific fun and always yields a great reward—FOOD, glorious food.

Your goal as an owner, therefore, is to be sensible about where food is placed in the home (and not much will be out of your

Blackie's reach!) and to reprimand your dog whenever he is caught in the act of stealing. But remember, only reprimand your dog if you actually see him stealing, not later when the crime is discovered; that will be of no use at all and will only serve to confuse him.

BEGGING
Just like food stealing, begging is a favorite pastime of hungry puppies! It achieves that same wonderful result—FOOD! Dogs quickly learn that their owners keep the "good food" for ourselves, and that we humans do not dine on dry food alone. Begging is a conditioned response related to a specific stimulus, time and place. The sounds of the kitchen, cans and bottles opening, crinkling bags, the smell of food in preparation, etc., will excite the dog, and soon the paws will be in the air!

Here is the solution to stopping this behavior: Never give in to a beggar! You are rewarding the dog for sitting pretty, jumping up, whining and rubbing his nose into you by giving him food. By ignoring the dog, you will (eventually) force the behavior into extinction. Note that the behavior is likely to get worse before it disappears, so be sure there are not any "softies" in the family who will give in to little "Oliver" every time he whimpers, "More, please."

INDEX

My Black Russian Terrier

PUT YOUR PUPPY'S FIRST PICTURE HERE

Dog's Name _____

Date _____ Photographer _____